A Leap to an Ecological Economy

Derek Paul

Archway Publishing books may be ordered through booksellers or by contacting:

Archway Publishing
1663 Liberty Drive
Bloomington, IN 47403
www.archwaypublishing.com
1 (888) 242-5904

ISBN: 978-1-4808-5171-9 (sc)
ISBN: 978-1-4808-5172-6 (e)

Library of Congress Control Number: 2017954766

Print information available on the last page.

Archway Publishing rev. date: 11/15/2017

Contents

The Book Cover

The cover of this book is the reproduction of an oil painting by the author. It is a metaphor for the book itself, namely, the transition from the known to the unknown, since nothing quite like an ecological economy has been tried out these last 300 years except on a local scale. The young ballerina in the picture, c. 1978, shoeless, wearing her school uniform and protected from the rain by an umbrella as she flies through the air, has already started the descent from her *grand jeté*. Her flight toward greener pastures can also be interpreted as a metaphor for the better human society that will result from a dynamic ecological economy. In this case, however, she does not know exactly what the terrain will be like when she lands (another piece of the metaphor), but land she must, and the rain adds to the uncertainty.

[The dancer is not related to the author.]

Acknowledgments

Robert Hoffman has most generously contributed to the aspects of this book concerned with modeling. Adam Newns' lively perceptiveness resulted in many improvements. David Millar's insights, wonderful good will and broad knowledge also led to improvements and new openings. Sam Lanfranco's generosity went beyond normal friendship, critiquing important chapters late at night after long summer days working on his farm. Louis Robichaud supervised my painting for the cover and was key to realizing the desired result. Julian Ortiz Cabrera provided insights I could not have obtained otherwise. Frank Feather's useful suggestions resulted, *inter alia*, in the added chapter on China. Above all, lilya Prim-Chorney, gave me much help and encouragement throughout the long journey, and kept reinforcing the notion that this book is urgently needed and must be published. To all the foregoing, I am intensely grateful.

I thank Metta Spencer and Adele Buckley for their rapid responses to calls for help. I also received encouragement from members of Coalition Climat Montréal, in particular Matthew Chapman, which is appreciated.

I thank Adrian Kuzminski warmly for his timely donation of a copy of his book, *The Ecology of Money*; and Sheila and Robert Murray for the gift of another book and, with Ted Mann, for a useful discussion and advice. Lastly, I thank Yves Bergeron for his rapid response on a question of afforestation, and for pointing me in the right direction.

Chapter One

Introduction

The purpose of this book is to outline the fundamental changes in economics that are necessary to bring the human race through its present series of crises. The most serious of the crises is long-term—namely, climate change. And it needs to be addressed now, because it is urgent (see Appendix 1) and people and governments have ignored the threat or set it aside for far too long. Numerous economists and other scholars have gradually recognized that climate change cannot be addressed within the traditional economy and, because of the urgency, it is vital to change economic thinking and practices. Because I want to develop the thread of new, ecological economics with a minimum of digression, the important subjects of climate change and other factors threatening humanity are mainly to be found in Appendices. Appendix 1 describes the most important facts of climate change, without entering into its immediate effects on today's world population. Appendix 2 provides some information on factors that can lead to the collapse of civilization, with projected dates under *laissez faire* for some critical shortages of supply; while Appendix 3 explains in rather simple terms the concept of ecological footprint; and thus provides a means for readers to assess from published footprint data the progress (or its opposite) in the human effort to render life sustainable.

The most important of the needed economic changes will lie deep in the minds of individuals everywhere—a change of paradigm. The word *paradigm* is often used loosely nowadays, to mean merely an idea or concept. But a paradigm is much more; it refers to a system of thought, and is the hidden skeleton upon which that system developed. Most people are not even aware of that skeleton, because they learned the system of thought within their family, and through contact with friends and teachers, and other influences including the media. Nobody ever mentions the origins of that thinking. But the classical paradigm, the classical framework that led to economic thinking, beginning in seventeenth-century Europe, is behind the development of the traditional economic system, as it operates today. It was not present everywhere in the world, but spread to increasing numbers of cultures as they acquired modern industry and the ideas that go with it. It will not be possible to change the economic system without changing the paradigm that underlies it, so we must look at the classical paradigm and also its necessary replacement. Phyllis Creighton and I wrote a paper on exactly this theme [1]. The following are the beliefs the classical paradigm rested upon [2]:

we must be rational and reject superstition;

humankind, being distinct from and superior to animals, has been given "dominion over" Nature and has the right and duty to control it;

growth (of industry, civilization etc.) is good *per se*, including human population growth;

technological progress is good *per se*.

In the new paradigm, only the demand for rationality remains from the old one, and at its center is the need to respect the Earth and sustain all of life in its fullness of diversity [1]. The new paradigm thus recognizes the interdependence of species, of which we humans are only one among very many. And here lies the clash between the old and the proposed new economics. While traditional economics allows us to exterminate cod, wolves and bees, and pump steers full of growth hormones, the new paradigm requires respect for life; and so must the new economics. Today's protesters against exterminations are part of the avant-garde in new thinking.

Of course the new paradigm isn't really new, since the aboriginal peoples have generally evolved to respect the Earth and its species, and many people even in western civilization have also done so; but these latter were not the drivers of the economic system.

The change in paradigm and therefore of attitude is now brought upon us by necessity because, if we don't change, we are done for. Some of the aboriginal sages of America have seen the collapse of western civilization as inevitable, while Canadian author Ronald Wright called the traditional economy a suicide machine [3].

The last three centuries have seen the economy in a state of evolution, with the adjective *neoliberal* applying to the phase since about 1980 when banking was much deregulated. This book is not an attempt to reverse the trends of the last 30 or more years, but to replace the entire gamut of variants of the economy that derived from the classical paradigm. I needed a word to describe these collectively, and chose *traditional*. But the word *neoliberal* will come up in these pages, especially when meaning the excesses of these last years.

With all of the above in mind, I completed half this work, and then discovered an important book by Hazel Henderson that is available on the internet: *Mapping the Global Transition to the Solar Age* (2014). In its 37 pages she covers a useful history of events, developments and ideas that tell very much of the mental changes taking place at high levels in industrial enterprises, with story after story of good things that are happening, many of them having enormous practical advantages for the world. I even went as far as thinking: *Has she said it all? Do I need to publish my ideas?*

I decided to proceed after all. Henderson's work is based upon continuing to use the present financial system and institutions, with new attitudes seeded within them. I see the ecological economy as requiring all of that plus a great deal of long-term wealth building, a few new instruments and practices, some legislation, and dramatic changes in at least one industry before it achieves the maturity that can address climate change successfully, and move the world more completely toward sustainability.

If this book generates controversy, then at least it will have opened important debates. The text is designed to prompt discussion both at the community and policy-making levels. Getting the best future means envisioning it and deriving the pathway from there to here.

Other threats

Climate change is by no means the only major threat to humanity. Much closer in time are threats such as collapse of civilization, global war, and collapse of individual national economies.

Avoiding a collapse of civilization requires the same prescription as facing up to climate change, which includes a major shift toward international cooperation.

Avoiding war, especially global war also requires a shift to cooperation, and away from confrontation and technological competition (see Chapter Eighteen). National economic failures must, for the time being, be dealt with individually, with understanding, generosity and, where possible, avoidance of major displacement of people.

What follows

Chapter Two outlines the character of traditional economics and why it must be replaced. Chapter Three lists fifteen respects in which an ecological economy must differ from the traditional one. Chapter Four is a primer on money, money creation and debt. Chapter Five explains the centrality of capital in economics and is a comment on what investment may be like in an ecological economy—in both senses of the word investment: investing resources and effort into making the economy sustainable, and investing money in stocks and shares. Chapters Six through Twenty outline what must or might be done to bring about a fully ecological economy. Then follow a chapter on China, inserted because of the importance of its economy and its equivocal situation with greenhouse gas emissions, and finally a chapter of recommendations.

Many of the notes refer to works written in the language of traditional economics, a thought process I try to avoid. But it's necessary to acknowledge good ideas, even if they come out of a decaying basket.

Notes

1. Derek Paul and Phyllis Creighton "A Holistic Paradigm for the 21st Century" 2008. This paper was presented as a poster at the 2004 International Conference on World Order at Ryerson University and subsequently updated: https://www.derekleverpaul.ca

2. The second and third of these statements are recognizable as biblical in origin. It helps when trying to understand the classical paradigm to recall that, in the days of Isaac Newton, nearly everyone in Christian western Europe took biblical statements as literally true.

It wasn't until Charles Darwin published his work on evolution that Christians slowly accepted that they were, after all, animals, albeit rather successful ones in the scheme of things. Current economics had its roots in that same age, along with the onset of banking. To a good approximation economics was carried forward by the classical paradigm until today. In these last decades increasingly many people have contributed to steer economics into new directions, recognizing the need for new thinking.

3. Ronald Wright *A Short History of Progress* 2004.

Chapter Two

Why the Traditional System Must Be Replaced

Several of my scientific colleagues recognized long before I did that the present economic system, which I shall call *traditional*, is doomed. The system, which is in principle (if not in fact) a free-enterprise, free-market system in which the chartered banks can literally create new money, has earned other names in the last forty years such as *neoclassical*, *neoliberal*, and *neoconservative*. But my colleagues called it *capitalism*, and stated that it must be replaced. Two of them felt that its replacement could only be achieved through violent revolution. I could not accept the notion of neoliberalism's violent overthrow on the grounds that the recovery time following such a revolution would exceed the time we have left in which to establish a sustainable economy and engage in the huge collaborative effort needed to face up to the threat of climate change. Regardless, therefore, of my personal abhorrence of violence and of the moral questions involved, a violent revolution would defeat the objective, namely, to replace the economy of waste with a sustainable system before it is too late. Others have argued privately that it is already too late, and civilization is doomed, but I reject that view because one of the few certainties about the future is that it will be full of surprises.

Many authors have made cogent cases against our traditional economy declaring it one of waste. Two books on the need for change in the economic system are important here, both of which refer to the earlier work in this field. Specific to the United States, Speth's *Another America is Possible* is one [2]; while Smith and Max-Neef's *Economics Unmasked* provide a broad, historical perspective [3]. The latter make a cast-iron case against the traditional economy and the urgent need to replace it, while Speth is equally thorough in his case against the current form of free-market economy, and all support their points with mountains of evidence. Philip Smith, in his chapters in *Economics Unmasked*, systematically points out how the traditional model contradicts itself and fails to match reality. Many of the arguments used by all three authors are based upon justice: what appears to be right and good for people and their natural environment. Given that traditional economics as practiced furthers the interests of the rich, and fails to advance the interests of the very numerous poor, the plight of the poor would seem to be of no consequence in traditional economic thinking. Were that not so, then the last forty years would have allowed plenty of time for the increasing inequalities in developed countries to be redressed. But the gap between rich and poor gradually increased during these last 45 years. This book is thus written on the basis that considerations of justice are unlikely to play a role in changing the system, from the standpoint of those currently in control [4]. The emphasis here is instead on the imminent collapse of the system [5]. Moral evils exist and would fully justify a profound change, even if collapse were not imminent; but we face that threat.

The objections to the present economic system have been voiced by many other authors. Briefly, the system is one that authorizes enterprises to pursue profit making without any built-in regard for resources; that is, as if resources are limitless, and as if the Earth can absorb any and all pollution that results from the system's operation. Therefore cost accounting has been based until now upon such direct elements as the financial cost of extracting a raw material (without regard to environmental damage done in the process) and the costs of manufacturing, without concern for where the products end up, which could be land-fill, lakes, rivers, the ocean, or the atmosphere.

There are many exceptions to the generalities just expressed, and some of these are beautifully recounted by Hazel Henderson [8], but the broad truth remains. When industries behave in the public interest, it is often because of regulation, not innate desire on the part of the corporation. Businesses detest being regulated, as is evidenced by recurring political efforts to bring about deregulation.

To facilitate comparison between the traditional economy of today and a fully ecological economy, the paragraphs that follow are labeled as in Chapter Three, which characterizes an ecological economy.

a) The traditional economy fails to **distinguish between money and wealth**, and measures wealth in terms of money. This follows from the assumption that money can buy anything, while ignoring that a desired good may have a value unrelated to money.

b) The traditional economy depends upon cheap labor for its maximum profit-making. It is easier to obtain labor when there is a shortage of available employment. At the same time, the economic system works better for the businesses when they can sell their products, implying that people have sufficient means to buy their products, and this occurs when employment is at a maximum. The compromise is a society enjoying moderately high employment, for example, one in which four to seven percent of the working population are seeking work. This changes, however, in times of recession, which are all too frequent and cause great hardship, as the employment drops radically. By contrast, full employment is never even talked about. I define it here as a situation in which all those who are able to work and who are seeking employment can at least find something. I hold that full employment is practicable, desirable, and essential for an ecological economy (see Chapter Seven). The traditional economic system has no built-in method of dealing with recessions, so that the people depend on outside interference, usually government action. An obvious action is for government to inject new money into the system in the hope of making it work, for example, to get the factories back into production, and restore the profit-making function of businesses, though these are only part of what needs to be done, and they don't make sense when there has been an overproduction of goods. The traditional thinking tends to lead to gross errors in the modes of stimulating the economy, as was seen after the crash in 2008. Following that recession very large sums of new money were created several times in the USA for the purpose of stimulating the economy, but very much of the money found its way into the "tertiary economy" [7], that is, the non-productive part of the economy. Thus a financial injection can have the effect of putting money primarily into the pockets of investors in that sector. Not nearly enough went into increasing prosperity across the entire US community. There are also historic examples of money creation where communities did receive benefit. President Roosevelt's

New Deal in the 1930s may be considered one of them, but it received much opposition from traditional business and economic thinkers.

c) The traditional economy shows no regard for the effects of its chosen pathways, such as basing its energy supply largely on burning fossil fuels, even though the results are extremely harmful to life on Earth. It continues to favor the petroleum industry, including governments rewarding corporations with subsidies, when renewable energy currencies are already available and preferable on important grounds.

d) The traditional economy encourages extraction of primary resources, maximizing their yield and industrial throughput, ending their trajectory as refuse or other forms of pollution.

e) Industrial and business practices, though excellent in more and more cases, lag behind what is needed for attaining sustainability, partly because of the legal basis of corporations. Highly undesirable practices include planned obsolescence and the deliberate destruction of surplus stocks that could be used elsewhere. The system measures economic success in terms of money, neglecting important factors in so doing.

f) The traditional system favors globalized markets, so as to increase trade, without regard for the overall economic benefit as reckoned with all environmental factors included, or when a broad-based comparison with local production is made.

g) The completely legitimate practice of advertising goods and services for sale, has, with the long-term assistance of focused psychological study, enabled the advertising industry to bring a large segment of human society into a state of obsession with consumer goods, sometimes amounting to an addiction to shopping. The evidence is the widespread practice of purchasing goods that are not needed by the purchasers or their families [8]. Such consumerism sustains the productive economy, but does so at the price of producing excess waste. Meanwhile, the economic system ignores real economic and sociological needs, such as maintaining infrastructure, the condition of the commons (see Chapter Fifteen), disenfranchised individuals and, to a large extent, the arts and artists.

h) Until 2010, legislation pertaining to the creation of new corporations in almost every jurisdiction held corporations responsible to their shareholders only for making profit. This narrow requirement for corporations stands out starkly as the only legal responsibility of corporate directors, a fact that has had many regrettable consequences. For example, a corporation may carry out its mandate leaving a seriously depleted environment around its work site. In states where the law tends to be enforced, much can be done through governmental regulation; this counteracts at least partly the deficiencies in their legislative basis. In poor countries, where, for example, the income provided by royalties on extracted ores can be desperately needed, environmental damage amounts to a loss of natural wealth suffered by the state. A shaft of new light appeared in 2010 with the creation of *benefit corporations* in a few US states (see Chapter Thirteen) a welcome departure from the long history of regulation and corporate efforts to achieve deregulation under traditional economics.

i) The banking system is in many ways exploitative, most often of people of low incomes, including students. Bank loans are almost always at considerable interest. The chartered banks themselves occupy a position of great privilege in western civilization, being the principal organs that have the right (in cooperation with a central bank) to issue new money, whereby they can make great profit. They also profit greatly from rapid international currency exchanges. Very few countries own their national banks, and these rarely use them to fund ecologically important projects.

j) The traditional system hasn't even come to terms with the concept of the *global commons* (see Chapter Fifteen). For example, the ocean and the ocean bed can surely be stated to be part of the global commons, but trawling has been allowed to wreak havoc there. Likewise, ocean fishing has not been regulated so as to assure future fish stocks, notwithstanding that at least 60 million people depend on fish for their protein, and that the maintenance of rich fisheries is thus essential.

k) Neoliberalism has nothing to say about global population, though population plays a proportional effect in almost all crucial issues facing humankind.

l) Businesses in food and agriculture have succeeded in feeding the rapidly expanding numbers of the human race, but this has been accomplished at a huge price. A whole new brand of agriculture has been developed based upon large monocultures of grain fed by chemical fertilizers, and assisted by massive application of chemicals to control pests. More recently, weed killers have been widely applied to prevent weeds taking nutrients from the soil that were placed there to feed the grain. The side effects of the pesticides are now known to be highly negative [8], and the glyphosate used as a weed killer has also been shown to be biologically dangerous [9]. Food industries have in addition degraded the food value of grain through industrial processes for grinding that remove the essential nutrients, while bread makers use techniques of leavening that fail to convert gluten into useful protein. Studies of vitamins and minerals in vegetables and fruit also indicate the decrease in food quality resulting from modern farming [8]. Many other factors affecting human health, rooted in the established medical profession and its accompanying drug industry, require attention: the separation of modern medicine from parallel professions; the neglect of great value in natural, herbal treatments. An integrative approach combining the best of both worlds, current-official and parallel, would have much to offer.

m) Militarism became a dominant, threatening factor in human life, following the arms build-up to WWI and reaching a new pinnacle in 1945 with the explosion of the first three nuclear bombs, two of which were dropped over Japanese cities. From then, militaries could count on huge support from governments, to develop a previously unimaginable range of new weapon systems. The political power of the military-industrial complex is widespread, to the point it can control some policies of universities that receive large military-related research contracts. Militarism, particularly in its latest form, fits well in the traditional economy, as it creates profit, employs many highly trained people, maximizes the throughput of resources, and is able to ignore the undoubted disadvantages it brings about. These last include extraordinary destruction, maiming and taking lives (mainly civilians), large-scale displacement of people, massive wastage of resources, and the fact that weapons sold abroad can later be used against the seller. All this fits with the form of accountancy employed, which measures everything in terms of money. Anatol Rapoport, a celebrated peace researcher, maintained that "None of the hypothetical aims of an offensive war bear critical scrutiny under contemporary conditions."

n) Traditional economics has enjoyed a period of unchallenged rule since the 1970s, and has given rise to an increasing gap in wealth between rich and poor throughout those years (see Chapter Nineteen).

o) The Gross Domestic Product (GDP) has been much criticized as an index for measuring and expressing prosperity, yet it is continually used and quoted, perhaps because of the simplicity of determining it.

Notes

1. Ronald Wright *A Short History of Progress* House of Anansi Press 2004.

2. James Gustave Speth *America the Possible: Manifesto for a New Economy* sales.press@yale.edu 2012.

3. Phillip Smith and Manfred Max-Neef *Economics Unmasked* Green Books 2011.

4. By contrast, justice is most important for citizens at large, and the struggle for justice is more and more evident from the activities of nongovernmental agencies and individuals. The need for justice could play an important role in bringing about an ecological economy.

5. The collapse could arise from acute shortages of essential goods (Appendix 2) or from militarism and war (Chapter 18), or a combination of these.

6. Hazel Henderson *Mapping the Global Transition to the Solar Age* internet 2014.

7. John Michael Greer *The Wealth of Nature: Economics as if Survival Mattered* New Society Publishers 2011.

8. Polly Higgins *Eradicating Ecocide* Shepheard-Walwyn (Publishers) Ltd 2010 Chapter 3.

9. The extensive and serious adverse health effects of glyphosate are fully explained with relevant evidence in Stephanie Seneff's 2013 video on YouTube:

https://www.youtube.com/watch?v=qYC6oyBglZI

Chapter Three

Characteristics of an Ecological Economic System

It is easiest perhaps to describe an ecological economic system by showing the ways in which it would differ from the system that is operating today. A focus, of course, is to ensure that the use of renewable resources does not impair future prosperity, and that the use of nonrenewable resources is carried on (as far as possible) with the same goal, implying a minimum of extraction and a maximum of recycling. In addition, the system must respect the Earth's capacities, and the health of the entire ecosphere. The transition from the old to the new economics presents many challenges, but the greatest of these is the widespread adoption of the new paradigm, especially in business, heads of industry, banking chiefs, and elected or appointed public servants and politicians who will be legislating and changing the rules where needed. The role of money will change from being the factor that controls what we may and may not do, into one that will instead facilitate achieving what urgently needs to be done. The relevant factors are discussed more fully in turn, in chapters six through twenty. Here is merely a current list of what I think an ecological economy (EE) must feature:

a) a clear distinction between wealth and money, and taking good care to increase wealth; assessment of wealth in terms of resources: natural, built and human capital; and accounting both nationally and by corporations in these terms

b) consistent full employment

c) an end to fossil-fuel burning

d) minimal extraction of primary resources, including trees, by maximizing recycling

e) the pursuit of ecologically sound goals in business and industry

f) a preference for local production, where beneficial; with changes in long-distance trade to match

g) a transformation of the advertising industry

h) more benefit corporations, with a legislative basis for them everywhere, and perhaps global standardization of their legal basis; and encouragement of other ecologically responsible enterprises

i) publicly owned banks (or equivalent machinery) in all single-currency areas, for funding what needs to be done in the EE context

j) clearly defined global commons, with formation and implementation of policies for their restoration or enrichment

k) sound population policies in all regions, with implementation of policy goals

l) increasing organic farming with a view to eliminating pesticides and herbicides for the sake of planetary health and improving food quality and nutrition; and rationalizing medicine integratively — for the improvement of human health

m) decreasing militarism and increasing international cooperation

n) a progressive reduction of social inequalities

o) new indices including capital wealth indices to replace GDP for assessment of prosperity and human welfare and the good state of the planet.

Items b) and i) through m) are particularly to be emphasized. Elaborating this slate of items with full justification of the separate points will likely be a work in progress for some time. The next seventeen chapters provide an introduction to money and investment followed by some ideas on how the fifteen requirements, a) through o) of the new system may be brought about. All of the material from Chapter Six on is preliminary, in that rather little of this long menu has yet been achieved anywhere, and there is always the need for more good ideas.

There are many organizations actively at work in this effort [1].

Note

1. The following is a list of centers, councils, foundations, institutes, and societies, all of whose names occurred somewhere in the researches for this book:

Centres/Centers

Development Alternatives Centre (CEPAUR)

Centre for International Cooperation

Centre for Sustainable Energy

Pulitzer Center

Steyer-Taylor Center for Energy Policy and Finance [at Stanford]

Councils

Canadian Mining Innovation Council

Conhar: Ireland's Sustainable Development Council

International Council on Mining and Metals

UK Energy Research Council

World Business Council for Sustainable Development

Foundations (Fdn)

Conservation and Research Fdn

Dag Hammerskjöld Fdn

Fdn for the Economics of Sustainability (FEASTA) [Dublin 1998]

Wangari Mathai Fdn

The New Economics Fdn

Institutes (Inst)

Global Carbon Capture and Storage Inst

Gund Inst for Ecological Economics [Vermont]

Inst for Ecomunicipality Education and Assistance

Inst for Economics and Peace (IEP)

Inst for New Economic Thinking

Natural Capital Inst [California]

Post-Carbon Inst

Product Policy Inst

Rodale Inst

Wangari Mathai Inst for Peace and Environmental Studies

Societies

The International Society for Ecological Economics (ISEE) and its various national branches

Chapter Four

Money and Debt

It will be important to have a rather good grasp of money and how it is created and how one can arrange to have enough in circulation to fulfill various requirements of a sustainable ecological economy.

In this chapter, we shall mainly be concerned with the government-approved official money that is used within countries and exchanged between countries. All manner of privately created money is possible, but I shall merely mention a couple of examples of parallel currency in Chapter Fourteen. What we must understand first is what the functions of our money are, how it is created, and why government has an essential role in maintaining its stability.

We use money primarily for our purchases (trade), for discharging debt, and we store it for later use, for example in savings accounts. Money also has symbolic value. In the complex society that most of us live in, the ability to exchange money into another currency is also important. This means that it is desirable that the relative values of different currencies not change too rapidly, otherwise traders could suffer huge losses, merely because a currency that they hold drops sharply relative to another that they use in their trading. Exchange rates are also influenced by capital flows and government engagement in foreign markets. Stabilizing the value of money and setting rules for its creation are matters for government and law.

Today, the concept of money is so familiar and dominant in people's minds, that we often forget that for millennia trade took place without official money. It would be hard to manage a complex economy without it! As things are it is vital to have some in one's pocket or bank account. But it comes with a price, since the supply and distribution of money in our very complex society often determine what happens, such as whether an important program goes ahead. Who controls money and on what terms is therefore vitally important.

Money and value

The former basing of value on metallic gold and silver arose from their properties: durability, verification through appearance and density measurement, and malleability for stamping coins of any size. As such they represented a standard of value for centuries. There is, however, no absolute standard of value, even though the investment community in our time does its best to create such a value by taking a weighted average of a range on national currencies.

One needs furthermore to distinguish between an exchange value (what someone can obtain for a good) and its use value (what that good was worth, or felt to be worth to that person).

Money creation and debt

Once government assumes the duty to control money, the next questions are the forms that money will take. The present forms of money are therefore not only legitimate in a moral sense as well as being legal, but the government undertakes to protect the public as far as possible through a variety of mechanisms, to which more can be added in times when currency is losing its value internationally, or threatens to do so. In the post-World War II years, when it was essential for Britain to prevent the pound sterling from dropping greatly in value relative to the US dollar, the British government prevented individuals from transferring more than 25 pounds into foreign currencies within a stated interval of time. This forestalled a likely devaluation of the pound during the repayment of the British war debt to the USA.

But where did the money come from in the first place? Was it all created by the national banks? Here the answer is astonishing: new money is created by the chartered banks, which are owned by shareholders. And banks create money when they make a loan [1]. Banks have a corporate basis much like any other corporation. And, when a bank creates new money, it simultaneously creates debt, the amount of the debt being exactly equal to the amount of newly created money. And here's the conservation law; if you take the debt to be negative money:

> the change in money plus the change in
> debt is exactly equal to zero.

There is a close analogy to this conservation law in the physical sciences, when electric charge is created. No positive electric charge can be created without simultaneous creation of an equal amount of negative charge.

Some economists argue that the total money plus total debt is zero and, while that is approximately true, it needn't be exactly true. I shall deal below with the dilemma of equality of amounts of money and debt, since it is an awful thought that in a prosperous economy with much money in circulation there need be as much debt. But, for discussion purposes, I shall assume that the total of money in circulation and in bank accounts ready for spending, is equal to the total debt owed by everyone.

A few national banks are owned by the government of their country, as are the Bank of Canada and the Bank of England [2], but most are corporations owned by their shareholders. In particular, the bank known as the federal reserve, which is the national bank of the USA, is privately owned, to the immense disadvantage of most of the people of that country [3]. The functions of the national banks include determination of the base rate of interest.

The circulation of money

When someone spends money it moves from one set of hands to another, and when those other hands spend it, it moves again. We can envisage money going from hand to hand until someone decides to use it to repay a bank loan. At that point, the money disappears and the same amount of debt disappears with it. If the individual repaid the debt in dollar bills, the bills don't disappear, but the individual's capacity to spend that amount disappears together with the debt. Such action takes money out of circulation. Part of the art of money control is to ensure that there is enough in circulation. In the early 1930s there was too little money in circulation in the USA, and there were very many unemployed who couldn't feed their families through want of money, a situation that eventually led to President Roosevelt's New (financial) Deal. By contrast, when the administrations of 2008 and subsequent years tried to warm up the economy, by putting huge sums into circulation, much of the money went into the hands of those who already had enough, and many simply invested it in speculative investments unconnected with production, sometimes called "the tertiary economy" [4]. Such money went out of circulation from the point of view of ordinary people, and circulated within the investment community, so the economic stimulus was slight, though it led to financial gains for certain investors. An advantage of giving such money to the poorest people is that one can be sure the money will all be spent locally, though this isn't necessarily the best way to stimulate an economy. Another failure of the kind of money creation we saw in those days was the bailing out of General Motors. Since General Motors only has responsibility to its shareholders, they did what might bring those shareholders maximum returns, and this has further reduced US prosperity (outside that circle of shareholders) by removing some centers of production away from the United States. Here I am not favoring any of the past methods of stimulating the economy, but rather stating what effects different types of distribution can lead to.

As we shall see, there is much to be done in the world that lies outside of traditional thinking, for which money will be required, but only as an agent, or helper.

In traditional economies, those who create new money acquire a degree of control of the economic system, but also they make great profit from their trade. In an ecological economy, much of the new money will be created to do things that will show no profit in the short term, and decisions to embark on such projects will have to be in the hands of those who best know the complete ecological picture, in particular how to address climate change. Thus one important role of money will be to facilitate vitally important projects at very low or zero interest, which will need a new mechanism for funding, far removed from current borrowing from a profit-making enterprise.

Debt burden

A potentially alarming thing about the monetary system is that the debt always equals the money. This means, in principle, that If I have cleared my debt and have a substantial positive net balance, then someone somewhere has debt in the amount of my prosperity (credit). I found that most depressing when I first recognized the truth of it. The apparent unfairness is, however, not a necessary feature of a monetary system, as can be understood by recognizing that the cause of grief is the debt burden, where the interest payable is crucial. In times of low interest rates the debt burden will be modest but, even in such times, very high rates of interest are charged by certain organizations for certain services. Perhaps interest on credit card debt is the most widespread example of legally allowed very high interest in our times, which are otherwise of low interest rates as I write. Yet people continue to use credit cards when they cannot afford the interest payments, so something is wrong here [5]. We have a fiscal system that disadvantages the most needy.

Debt and interest rates have been very extensively discussed within the traditional economy. The trends within the economy for the last 35 or more years have led to cumulatively increasing debts of governments in the developed world as well as of individuals, and has given rise to insolvency in several spectacular cases. One example will suffice. The national debts in Europe increased dramatically on average since the formation of the European Union, most critically in the poorer countries. Overall, the reason was the agreement at the time of foundation of the Union that governments would not be permitted to borrow at low interest from their central bank, but only from the chartered banks, whose interest rates were significantly higher than that of the central bank. This misjudgment by the founders of the European Union presumably could have been avoided had they modeled the system in advance to project a financial future. The picture of how western governments have allowed themselves to get into debt and now must generate huge budget surpluses just to pay the interest, has been excellently and succinctly described by Louis Gill [6].

Prime and other rates of interest

Wikipedia gives us a general definition:

"Prime rate or prime lending rate is a term applied in many countries to reference an interest rate used by banks. The term originally indicated the interest rate at which banks lent to favored customers—i.e., those with good credit—but this is no longer always the case. Such interest rates may be expressed as a percentage above or below prime rate."

The prime rate can be changed by the governor of the national bank following a committee decision, a matter of great concern to businesses and investors.

Other rates sometimes advertised by banks are often called base rates, such as a base rate of interest on line-of-credit accounts, of for mortgage loans. Implicitly, the rate of interest charged to the borrower may be higher than the base rate.

Money in ecological economy

Let's now look at an ecological economy, one in which we intend to address the emergency of climate change. It will be necessary to make money available for many projects at nominal (meaning negligible) interest. The idea of interest-free loans (printing more money) isn't new. It was used by Canadian Prime Minister McKenzie King to finance Canada's role in WWII. He just asked the Bank of Canada to provide the funds as needed. At the end of the war, the debt was large, but the debt burden small; and the Government owed the money to itself! There are also chartered banks that offer interest-free loans today [7], but not necessarily on the scale that will be required in the future economy.

Issuing interest-free money necessarily raises the question, "is the project worth it?" And this is bound to be a recurring question in an ecological economy. But it cannot and must not be answered using the criteria of the traditional economy, because that is the system that has brought the ecosphere to its present low point. This is also the reason Edward Kellogg's monetary system is mentioned below.

The rate of interest required for special projects such as addressing climate change will likely have to be nominal or zero. By contrast, commercial banks make a substantial fraction of their income from interest on loans, so we would be wise to anticipate a dual banking system, which is recommended in this book.

"Printing more money" happens to have an advantage that it puts more money into circulation. Thus, if we discount the debt that carries no interest, we arrive at a compromise where the money in circulation is greater than the debt (meaning the interest-carrying debt), and this could be an overall advantage in any creatively new economy [8]. The immense indebtedness of North Americans today (2017) has been much deplored, as it invites widespread bankruptcy.

Principles in New Economics

In 1999 I presented a paper—at the international World Order Conference at Ryerson University—in search of a superordinate principle, which I ended up calling "The Principle of Life." What I found was that the adoption of the new paradigm (see Chapter One), based upon taking planetary life as a value, amounts to such a superordinate principle, from which very many sub-principles can be derived. For example, all the 26 ecological principles emerging from the UN's Declaration on the Human Environment (1972) are sub-principles of this central principle. So is the *Golden Rule*, that is, the idea that one should treat others as we would like them to treat us, plus its extension from individuals to groups and nations. In fact the United Nations itself is the first manifestation of the extended principle. When it comes to economics and money, some sub-principles are easily derived:

1. Loans, especially to poor people or poor countries must be made on terms that render them repayable without unacceptable social cost. [It could turn out to imply that such loans would have to be made at nominal interest by national banks.]

2. It is not the business of any lending agency to determine the social policy in a borrower country. Such interference violates the Principle of Life.

Banking structure and interest rates in an ecological economy

Likely this in untrodden ground, so let's make a start. The choices of system will range within the following extremes:

a) modifying the present system so that funds are plentifully issued by publicly-owned banks (which would need to be created where there are none) at nominal interest for ecologically important projects, leaving the banking system we now have minimally altered;

b) creating a dual system, in which there are new, publicly owned banks to finance the ecological projects as in a) and a new banking system to do the rest.

A useful study on interest rates comes from Edward Kellogg's posthumously published book, *A New Monetary System*, 1861. The key idea was a decentralized and thus locally controlled monetary system based upon a fixed interest rate of 1.1 percent [9]. His choice of 1.1 percent was based upon the notion that this would produce interest over a 60-year period equal to the capital, and that higher rates of interest placed undue pressure on the borrower. Although Kellogg's proposed monetary system is completely different from anything people are familiar with today, the basis of low interest and steady value of money are attractive; though Kellogg's system would likely suffer some buffeting in a system where large sums are created in parallel for increasing natural wealth and addressing climate change.

Watching the balance

Such action as financing major projects at nominal interest requires careful oversight, as the economy can run into major inflation. However, there are several methods of preventing this, including debt repayment through taxes. In an ecological economy with full employment, there would not likely be privation as a result.

This discussion is continued in Chapter 14.

Notes

1. When you borrow from a bank, it is generally not possible to determine how much of the borrowed money is new money and how much was already on deposit at that bank; but at the end of a year, one could study what the average amount on deposit had been, and compare it with the net amount outstanding in loans. Typically in Canada and the United States, the outstanding loans would exceed the amount on deposit by a factor of about 30, indicating that 29/30 of the borrowed money is new money. By contrast, credit Unions

are not entitled to create new money, which means they cannot loan money in excess of what they have on deposit.

2. The Bank of England claims as its mission: "to promote the good of the people of the United Kingdom by maintaining monetary and financial stability." www.bankofengland.co.uk

3. The huge advantage of a country having a publicly owned national bank is that when the government borrows from its bank it owes the debt to itself (or the nation). This doesn't mean that loans can be drawn without serious thought, since there is always the question of how much money there should be in circulation, and great excesses can give rise to unwanted inflation, and loss of value of the currency.

4. John Michael Greer *The Wealth of Nature: Economics as if Survival Mattered* New Society Publishers 2011 pp.59-68.

5. Banks sometimes offer a lower-than-normal interest rates on credit card debt to low-income clients and allow a low limit to that debt. This sounds generous, but exceeding the debt limit can, instead of causing the client to be refused further credit, incur a financial penalty. In the short term, the penalty can amount to an exceptionally high interest rate.

6. Louis Gill "Les dettes souveraines et la domination des marchés financiers" (translation: "Sovereign debts and the dominance of financial markets") in *Sortir de l'économie du désastre* eds Bernard Elie et Claude Vaillantcourt Méditeur 2012 pp. 77-89.

7. Examples are the JAK Bank in Sweden and, worldwide, the Islamic banks, notably in Dubai and Pakistan where the largest is the Meezan Islamic Bank.

8. Some authors have used the expression *debt money* to mean money created at interest, and therefore giving rise to debt burden.

9. A discussion of Kellogg's work can be found in Adrian Kuzminski's book *The Ecology of Money* Lexington Books 2013.

Chapter Five

Capital and Investment

The failure of almost everyone alive to distinguish between money and wealth is understandable. The human race has lived for over 300 years with an economic system and a banking system that blur the distinction, because it has been assumed all that time that money could buy anything if you had enough of it. Moreover, this was usually the case. However, money cannot buy anything that is simply unavailable, no matter what that something is. After large diameter tree trunks have all been cut down and used industrially, money will not buy you any more, though you may take steps to ensure a supply some eighty years ahead. Traditional economists continue to support their obsolete system by saying, "well, if there isn't enough wood, we'll, find a substitute material." [1] This applied across the board (pun intended), to whatever resource is becoming scarce. The response to freshwater shortage is to desalinate the ocean locally, and pump the newly produced fresh water to where it is needed. Both processes are energy intensive, and the desalination is usually polluting in one or more ways, implying that some other resource is being degraded. The degradation of the biosphere through any of these polluting processes represents a loss of wealth, but the accountants within the traditional system are not obliged to compute such effects or to present them in their balance sheets. The accounting is done in terms of money, while the incidental losses of wealth, often of natural wealth, are overlooked no matter how large they are.

A major problem facing the human race is therefore to relearn the important difference between money and wealth, which will bring with it the understanding that one must measure wealth in natural units. The National Roundtable on The Environment and the Economy (NRTEE) did Canadians a great service at the end of the last millennium when it produced a set of wealth indices for the federal Department of Finance [2]. The government hoped thereby to be warned when a natural resource was declining dangerously. No doubt this was prompted by the shock of the collapse in ocean cod stocks late in the 20th century. For a time it looked as if that important resource would disappear entirely, and the Finance Department thought that indices might give useful future warnings. NRTEE produced the desired system of indices, and all of them were given in natural units, such as estimated numbers (or tonnages or volume) of fish, lumber, etc.

As part of its work on these indices, NRTEE recognized three types of capital: natural, built and human. The natural capital was mostly what their index system addressed. Built capital meant wealth that the human race constructs, such as buildings and bridges, objects that have a certain permanence. The human capital is designed to measure the usefulness to human society of its own people, through education and training and their overall capabilities. One can put dollar values on any of these things, but they don't mean much, as they could vary tremendously from day to day, whereas a building that will house six families will presumably have the same value to its users and to society as a whole from one week to the next in the absence of disaster, and provided there is good maintenance.

These notions of capital are fundamental and system-independent to the extent that they refer to any human society trying to attain or sustain prosperity on this planet. They are therefore basic to any economic system. The creation of an economic system therefore involves the question of who will control or own these capital assets and how they will be managed and used to bring about the desired prosperity.

Predictably, the human mind has invented systems that range from one extreme to another: from a maximum of sharing between people, to control by a centralized authority, or to a free-for-all system allowing individuals to accumulate capital and power for themselves. At the extreme of maximal sharing we have the example of the aboriginal people in North America, who not only shared resources within their tribe, but also took care not to overexploit those resources, thus ensuring the sustainability of their system. The system included conventions about trespassing on the territory of neighboring tribes, which could lead to serious friction. But within the tribal lands the system worked well.

Among technologically more advanced societies we have the extreme control of the communist regimes that insisted on natural and most or all built capital being the property of government, while the rest of the industrial world wanted it in "private" hands, which of course has included the hands of powerful corporations. Countries with the capital in "private" hands are not necessarily democratic. Reading Placide Gaboury's delightful book, *Petite Galerie de Grands Esprits (Small Gallery of Great Minds)*, I was struck by his mention of the four types of government recognized by Plato: oligarchy, democracy, military dictatorship and tyranny [3], and that Plato condemned them all. In my lifetime, it has seemed that democracy was the best, as objectively it has handled environmental concerns less badly than the others, and has protected human rights up to a point. But it has revealed many flaws in other respects, particularly in the failure of elected representatives to represent the views of those who elected them. So we might do well to pay attention to Plato's condemnation. But what else is there that might govern a new, ecological economy? Here I am groping in the dark, but believe there may be hope in some form of participatory democracy [4]. That also will likely not be enough, since we need a political framework in which decisions must somehow be evidence-based.

Few governments, if any, have dealt satisfactorily with the question of capital, who should own it and on what terms. The basic political problem is that private ownership can lead to too much exploitation, while public ownership is rarely if ever transparent enough. Capital can be held by government to follow its own whims, without it being held truly on behalf of the people.

What then might work in an ecological economy? To answer this even partly, one does well to examine what has been happening in human civil society these past 30 or more years. Two big economic changes since WWII in western society have been the advance in universal public health care (with the noted exception of the United States) and the increasing expectation of employees that they will receive pensions upon retirement. Public health care is a major expense for governments, though it only partly justifies the current high taxation rates in the countries that have it. The pensions, by contrast, need returns on investments to pay the huge annual bill.

Investment is inevitably tied to capital, in the sense that all elements of capital in an economy must either be held by one or a defined group of individuals or held in common. I suggest that investment by pension funds is an unavoidable consequence of human expectations in the current age, and that the major pension funds will be a feature of any economy that we could realistically envision. But this will not exclude government from intervention for the sake of social justice. Also I think that private investment by individuals and other investment groups will continue. Most important for a new, ecological economy will be to encourage employee-investment, so that the proportion of industry or a business owned by the employees will increase. The increase of ownership of enterprises by employees is discussed nicely by Alperovitz for the United States, where many Employee Stock Ownership Plans (ESOPs) have been developed [5].

But what then must be the changes in investing? Obviously investing must have a role in steering the economy toward sustainability. The good news is that this is already starting to happen.

Matthew Kiernan has brought to light and emphasized the importance of environmental and social (ES) considerations in investment, pointing out that the trends toward sustainability are increasingly evident in corporate policy. In chapter 4 of his book [6], he presents evidence from a series of studies indicating better average performance of stocks when the companies take sustainability seriously and manage their affairs accordingly. This shows up in investment returns when portfolios (consisting of many stocks) are assessed in terms of sustainability ratings, which Innovest (Kiernan's former company) did routinely. One can then look at how an actual portfolio is doing and assess how it would have performed had the stocks been weighted according to sustainability ratings. On average, such studies lead in about 85 percent of cases examined by Kiernan to potentially or actually enhanced performance of the portfolio having the sustainability weightings. The negative aspect of his findings was that, in that same period, most portfolio managers in the investment business refused to consider sustainability ratings in their assessments of stocks. Now, however, Kiernan sees increasing numbers of those same managers having come around to include sustainability ratings in the weightings within the portfolios they put together (private communication, February 2017). This is very good news.

Further political questions

The history of Western civilization has an abominable record on theft of capital, as was exhibited following the decline of the Middle Ages and entry into the Renaissance and then the Age of Reason. People well placed in society were empowered to take over what had been common land and claim ownership to it. An analogous wealth grab occurred, though much faster, at the demise of the Soviet Union, at which time all capital was the property of the State, except for a few dachas and some trivial items, amounting to a negligible portion of the whole. When the USSR broke up, the most valuable built assets, such as the oil industry, were systematically grabbed, in what must be the greatest theft in history. The theft of private property by the Soviets in 1917 was also impressive, but at least that was done in the name of the public and ostensibly for their benefit. One of the many Soviet failures was that members of the public were not given shares as legal evidence of their ownership of what was held in common for them by government. The same can be said of any western government that holds wealth on behalf of the public. This same lack has been characteristic of government takeovers of capital assets everywhere, including in so-called democratic countries.

Democratic government has further failed in its grasp of public versus private interests, in that, when it has accumulated a property or business concern in the name of the public, it always retains the right to sell it back to private interests. There has been nothing to stop government in acquiring assets at very great cost and selling them into private hands at a much lower total price. Maybe some shares should not be tradable, but instead held by each taxpayer for his or her lifetime. We also hear too often of the privatization of water supplies, going even as far as making it illegal for people to collect water from their own roofs [7]. Such absurd and unjust occurrences could in principle be prevented if publicly owned properties, enterprises and facilities were literally owned non-transferably by the public, who would themselves be the shareholders. Water resources must surely become part of such commons. The above dilemmas, as well as the more obvious ones, such as tax loopholes for the rich, are some of the areas where the ecological economy will have to improve markedly upon what we have today.

Next we must look at the kinds of shares that are available on the stock market, many of which involve ownership of enterprises producing goods and materials that are widely valued and used, while others include businesses such as stores, that also fulfill important social functions. Then there are the banks. All such enterprises must be owned by someone or some named group, or held in common by the public. There is nothing wrong in principle with investment. Even Marxists believe in it, though they think (or used to think) that all enterprises should be publicly owned.

Most investment, private or public, is risky. The most soundly run business can collapse through unpredictable developments. Therefore investors must seek protection from such risk by diversifying their investments. On the positive side, there can be huge profit from wise investment. With private investment, a difficult question is how much of that profit should return to government, having regard to the risk element and other factors, and this question is reasonably dealt with in many jurisdictions. With regard to the ethics of investment, I again refer readers to the works of Hazel Henderson [8].

There are established developments in the stock-trading world, in which the "products," such as derivatives, have nothing to do directly with production. This question is discussed by John Michael Greer who refers to this sector of investing as the "tertiary economy" [9]. He points out that, following the 2008 crash, many of the billions in new money put into the economy to stimulate economic activity in fact went into this tertiary economy, which is essentially unconnected with the production of goods and services to satisfy human needs, so that the investment is pure gambling. This tertiary economy has reached a scale within the current investment system such that it needs prompt attention. The basic reason is that it drains money from circulation in the first and second economies, which include all economic activities directly affecting human wellbeing. At the same time it enriches some of those who invest in it and benefits nobody else, though it circulates a huge amount of money within itself. It thus blurs the apparent amount of money in useful circulation for normal productive and trade purposes, since it drains much of it off to one specialized part of the stock market.

In conclusion, I think that investment in productive enterprises will likely proceed similarly in an ecological economy as it does today, but with an increasing focus on sustainability of enterprises that investors are willing to invest in. The tertiary economy would appear to require special new regulations, perhaps including taxation, to keep the money circulating within it in some ratio to the amounts circulating in the primary and secondary economies (Greer's terminology) [10]. I can see no objection to public ownership of capital, provided that it is truly public, and not merely held by government. For vital supplies, such as fresh water, it would seem obvious that public ownership must prevail.

Notes

1. A useful but by no means conclusive discussion of substitution and other related economic concepts can be found in Daly and Farley's *Ecological Economics* second edition chapter 5.

2. National Roundtable on the Environment and the Economy (NRTEE) *Environment and Sustainable Development indicators for Canada* Renouf Publishing Ltd 2003 ISBN 1-894737-06-7. The Introduction includes the following statement: The development of these indicators is founded on the new economics that recognizes that the world's natural capital provides us with services that are crucial to society. I warn readers that the expression *new economics* is also used nowadays to refer to the manner in which traditional economics has developed since the 1970s, though this is clearly not what is meant in NRTEE's statement.

3. Placide Gaboury *Petite Galerie de Grands Esprits* Quebecor 2002.

4. Dmitri Roussopoulos and C George Benello eds *Participatory Democracy* Black Rose Books 2005. Hazel Henderson *Building a win-win World* Berrett-Koehler Publishers 1996 chapter 11.

5. Gar Alperovitz *America beyond Capitalism: reclaiming our wealth, our liberty and our democracy* democracy collaborative press 2011 chapter 7.

6. Matthew J Kiernan *Investing in a Sustainable World* Amacom 2009.

7. The acquisition of water rights by corporations can take place and has done so in numerous countries, whether through urgent need of funds by the government concerned or through corruption. Such decisions would be almost unthinkable under participatory democracy.

8. Hazel Henderson *The Politics of the Solar Age: Alternatives to Economics* Knowledge Systems Inc 1988. Chapter 13 "Thinking Globally, Acting Locally: Ethics for the Dawning Solar Age" encapsulates Hazel's very general thinking on the transformation that must come.

9. John Michael Greer *The Wealth of Nature: economics as if survival mattered* New Society Publishers 2011.

10. John Michael Greer *loc.cit.* In Greer's scheme, pp. 59-61, primary goods and services are defined as those provided by Nature, while secondary goods and services involve human labor. By contrast the tertiary economy is the provision of monetary goods and financial services, "that in theory foster the distribution of the products of the primary and secondary economies, but in practice . . . obscure crucial trends in the first and second economies behind a fog of paper wealth."

Chapter Six

Assessment of Wealth and Wealth Creation

The necessity of increasing natural capital arises especially from the losses due to human plundering of the natural world, for example, farming that gives rise to a dust bowl. The desecration of the natural world, in combination with the huge increase in human population, is fast reducing the probability of a happy next chapter to the human story. But the possibility of a happy next chapter remains, and depends on rebuilding what has been destroyed or allowed to decay, **and on keeping the peace while this is going on**.

A few projects will serve to typify how to increase natural wealth in today's context and increase the probability of feeding the billions who will be craving food thirty years from now.

Biochar

There's an increasing awareness of the potential role of biochar for making infertile soil more fertile. Biochar is a relative newcomer in the art of soil fertility improvement, and will play the role of an additive, rather than a replacement for previously known methods. Biochar is the residue from organic matter that has been cooked at high temperature in an atmosphere free of oxygen [1]. The carbon residues from the heating have crevices of molecular dimensions that can store water or nutrients, making them invaluable for water retention in drought, and in improving soils generally through the retention of nutrients.

Today's biochar proponents see it as an agent for improving agriculture and maintaining or improving the quality of forest soil. To realize these benefits the biochar must be manufactured on the needed scale, a considerable task when dealing with large acreages. Producing biochar and applying it to farm or forest adds to natural wealth through increased agricultural productivity or tree growth, and can help to preserve biodiversity, by accommodating more individuals of most given species. Soil improvement is expensive in its requirements for the necessary material resources (biochar, mulch, and possibly minerals) and labor, though the labor element may also be viewed as a benefit, since the present economy generally leaves too many unemployed. The benefits will take time to show net profit from improved crops because of the substantial initial outlay. This time delay is a feature of all the wealth-increasing projects suggested in this chapter. In forest, there is a relatively early benefit from CO_2 sequestration, which will occur long before saplings have grown to maturity. Appendix 4 expands on benefits of biochar in addressing climate change through increasing carbon sequestration.

2. Cleaning river systems

This is something the human race does know how to do, but too rarely does it to the needed degree. Run-off from agriculture is an important example of how a river gets polluted, and it can be reduced by planting trees or bushes along the river banks. Muddy rivers can be changed into clear waterways and the run-off of pesticides and fertilizers can be hugely cut down if not eliminated. There is a loss of agricultural area by virtue of the planting, but there can be economy in the amount of fertilizer required, and increased productivity if biochar is used with a view to retention of the fertilizers.

An ambitious project, not yet achieved after many years of effort, is the cleaning of the Mississippi-Missouri river system, which spans a huge area reaching as far as north mid-western Canada [2]. The Mississippi discharges its water into the Gulf of Mexico, where it has created a dead zone, one of the largest in all the world's ocean at almost 18,000 square km in 2015 [3]. The ocean dead zones are areas so deprived of oxygen that fish and mammals formerly commonplace there cannot live within them. A major benefit from cleaning up the Mississippi will be to restore that huge area to living ocean, eventually providing fisheries. The process of coming back to life of an ocean dead zone may be slow, but it would seem a crime not to attempt it, while to do nothing is like accepting that the Earth is dying. But there would also be benefits for the agricultural and forest areas affected, and the quality of the land is critically important in our highly populated world. The work force needed to achieve these objectives might be large, another benefit in the economy of full employment (see Chapter Seven).

The Mississippi basin project and the failure of conservation efforts so far illustrate very nicely the difference between a traditional approach and a fully ecological approach. In the former, a sum of money (if available) is thrown at the problem. In the latter, a full study would be made to assess what needs to be done to succeed, and then the plans are made to go assemble the needed resources and team management and move forward. It could be, in the Mississippi basin case, that much of the farming in some areas would additionally have to be converted to organic in order to succeed fully, and that other crucial changes be made in other areas, such as widespread use of biochar as suggested above. The object here is, however, not to try to solve the problems by guesswork, but to hint at elements of ecological strategy.

The evidence from the National Geographic's 2014 article [3], is that there are also contributions from cities to the contamination of the Mississippi's waters, which further complicate the full solution.

At the end of the above planning processes, the big question is, "Is it worth doing?" And the answer is almost certainly "yes," because we are living in an overcrowded world, and it's going to get harder to keep things productive and unpolluted all the time that population keeps growing, so it's surely worth learning how to achieve this. And the Mississippi basin is a great test case.

The likelihood of a large labor requirement for a project such as this is again no barrier in an ecological economy, except when there is a temporary labor shortage, but that would surely be local, and no real obstacle.

3. Afforestation

Forest creation where there is none–afforestation–is another scheme for increasing natural wealth that will show no early profit, but will increase natural capital and sequester CO_2 while doing so, two vital factors in the essential global future.

Afghanistan was recognized by an official in Ontario's forest service as a great area for afforestation, having the right soil and water conditions over a considerable area [4]. There is no shortage of labor in Afghanistan, where the human problem is more likely to be that of persuading people to lay down their arms so as to participate in the work. This strategy of wealth production is also linked with the first. Afforestation elsewhere, especially in desert areas is of particularly great interest. The big questions are soil quality and water availability. In some areas, such as the Dalmatian coast, which was stripped of its trees centuries ago, the rainfall might just be sufficient for afforestation, but the soil eroded long ago into the Adriatic, and would have to be replaced. The labor and energy costs of such a project would be large, unless some new system was invented to rebuild the soil and supply sufficient water to the young forest until it became reestablished. An advantage of such a project could be an improvement of the Mediterranean rainfall, at least in the general region of reforested areas. Indeed, the Mediterranean basin has suffered much from past deforestation.

An example of a semi-desert that has been converted into a tropical forest these last 55 years is Auroville, in south-east India, a few km west of Pondicherry. Auroville's forest was planned only in the sense that settlers who went there, having obtained a substantial area of land, began early on to search for underground water. Having found water, they then planted trees as and where they felt inclined. The area is now regarded as tropical forest by many, though of course it has the monsoon in season.

Analogous forest creation is possible in many places, though not necessarily easily in most, soil and water being primary questions.

The Great Green Wall of Trees to Halt the Sahara

For this important project, refer to recommendation 7d and note 7d in Chapter Twenty-Two.

Afforestation in the north

The tree line is the long, irregular east-west curve running across northern Canada and much of Russia north of which trees, even rather small, stunted trees, are not found. Global warming has moved the potential limit for trees to flourish a great deal further north than today's actual tree line. A decade ago estimates of the possible extension were 100-150 km further north than in the mid-twentieth century. Today, with arctic ice disappearing, the tree line could move northward until the forest reaches the tundra. Thus there is a potential of extending tree growth over more than a million square km in northern Canada and Russia.

The natural growth northward of trees is slow compared with what is desirable for a major increase of carbon sequestration, but it is occurring, and could be accelerated by planting. However, the farthest-north boreal forest is particularly subject to forest fires (Prof. Yves Bergeron, private communication 2017). An optimization of its potential benefit would thus need some study and planning in terms of fire control in very remote areas.

Land-use planning for a sustainable future

In North America, land-use planning has mostly seemed to be based upon short-term thinking, or rapid profit-making for development, with the result that in some regions much useful agricultural land has been built over, especially in the more fertile agricultural areas. Up until now, the consequences have not been severe, in the sense that there have been continental food surpluses in many if not all the years during which such building development has been surging ahead. Looking far enough forwards, the picture changes drastically. The large human populations are still increasing; several megacities are still expanding; and good farmland is still being lost to development in many areas, while rainfall patterns are changing, implying that farmland is bound to become more important in those areas where the rainfall remains plentiful.

At the same time, there are considerable areas not suitable for agriculture that would be suitable for building and manufacturing. The immediate need, therefore, is planning with a 30-year forward vision, which takes us into the decade 2040-2050, likely to be one of scarcity (see Appendix 2).

The ecological economy will have to do a much better job of planning than the traditional economy has done.

Notes

1. The intense heat in the preparation of biochar drives off all the other molecules in the organic matter, and breaks them down into simple compounds. Some noxious compounds can be produced, but these can be destroyed by an after-burner. For further discussion of biochar, see Appendix 4.

2. The US Government provided USDA with $320 million (USD) for this project in 2009. The 12 April 2014 issue of National Geographic published Brian Howard Clark's article "Mississippi Basin Water Quality Declining Despite Conservation."

3. The National Center for Coastal Ocean Science "2015 Gulf of Mexico Dead Zone 'above average'" 4 August 2015.

4. Ontario Forest Service, personal communication, 2007.

Chapter Seven

Maintaining Full Employment

In a society maintaining full employment, it will not necessarily mean that everyone is working, but it should mean that anyone looking for a job should be able to get one within days, even if it isn't exactly what she/he was looking for.

That approximation in fact occurred in post-WWII Britain in some places where factories were fully occupied in the trade boom following the war. In one city where the unemployment rate was 0.5 percent the unemployed were described as those in the process of changing jobs. Nobody who wanted work needed to be unemployed for more than a few days.

An obvious reason for maintaining full employment is its social desirability; it removes the awful uncertainty that one can be deprived of being able to provide for oneself or others, possibly having to face great want. The traditional economic system provides less than full employment nearly all the time, and recurring periods of severe unemployment in its recessions. In poorer countries unemployment is often very high; while starvation has too often been the result of displacement or drought, etc. In April 2017, a news article announced the lowest unemployment figure for the European Union in many years—slightly over nine percent. If that is a low unemployment rate for good times, then something is surely wrong with the economic system.

Comparative economic studies show that of all age groups the one from 18-30 suffers the worst in the Canadian economy, and it must be obvious why, given that it has the least political clout of the adult groups, while younger groups have parental and legal economic protection. Opportunities for youth must therefore rank high in the new economy, since these young people are humanity's future. What chance is there for a healthy future if they are set aside? A good start will be full employment opportunity, and education without resulting debt burden and, if possible, entirely without resulting debt.

Depression caused in part by the unemployment was emphasized in a recent article in *Le Devoir* [1], with the title (translated) "Depression hits young Canadians hard." The article reveals that in 2012 no fewer than 150 thousand Canadians between ages 15 and 24 made suicide attempts.

An objection to full employment from an industrial standpoint can arise from the poorer selection of people available when there is a vacancy to be filled, but I believe this can be compensated by careful planning in the education/training sector. I also believe that this will take care of itself in an economy of extensive ecological projects, where many of those engaged in such projects are likely to be young adults, among whom suitably qualified individuals would in principle be available to enter industries at any time as industrial requirements arise. People engaged in such projects might also include highly qualified individuals who were temporarily without employment requiring their qualifications.

What of the transition from the old economy to the new? It will be essential to increase employment throughout the transition, or go for full employment at the outset and maintain it, because any severe drop in employment could bring about enough social unrest to halt the transition. And that is the second reason for full employment, to assist in the transition.

Fundamental economic changes will lead to social stress and protest if there are job losses. And it is obvious that changing from an energy base of coal, oil and natural gas would cause extensive job losses in those sectors. The coal and oil industries will not close, because these resources are needed for the manufacture of chemicals, plastics and fibers, but the burning would cease, and this will immensely reduce employment in those industries. Curiously, the profit over the lifetime of a mine or oil well will not necessarily suffer, and might even rise, but it will be realized over a very much longer period; and the human race will benefit overall, because these primary resources are needed in the long term, and could otherwise be reduced to nil (or uselessness) within 100 years. The problem of producing clothing for billions of people without oil and coal had obviously not been thought out, else the industries might not have worked so hard to prevent action to address climate change. It has often struck me as strange that these industries have worked so hard against their own and humanity's best long-term interests. But again, that is brought about by the system itself.

If old jobs are disappearing, where will the new jobs be, and can we employ everyone capable of working?

Modern industry can produce all the manufactured goods needed by the human race with fewer and fewer people as time passes, because of increasing automation and the use of robots. In principle, robots save humans from having to do dull repetitive work and on that basis are considered a general good. But there are limits to this advantage, that go beyond the time and space for discussion here. Briefly, the value of robots in industry is related to the corporate taxation structure, which is ill thought out, to say the least, in the traditional economy. Robots do not need to be a barrier to employment in a well planned and well run economy.

To create the new jobs we must go beyond traditional, industrial thinking. There will be and are already increasing job opportunities in the renewable energy industries, and there are always opportunities in the service industries, but these will not go far enough to bring about full employment. We could guess that at best they will lead to a job situation only slightly better than we have now.

Many of the new jobs will therefore be generated in the general field of natural wealth creation (see Chapter Six), including restoring the commons and building and maintaining infrastructure. New jobs will also be created in education. The basic reasons are as follows. Restoring or enriching the commons increases natural capital, which is of huge long-term concern for all life, including human life. Creating and maintaining infrastructure increases built capital [2]. Education increases human capital, highly relevant to human prosperity and overall wealth. These three forms of wealth are the fundamental bases of the economy as it needs to be.

Note that an ecological economy would not expect to increase employment by increasing industrial production in the developed countries, where many people have more *things* at home than they can comfortably house.

I believe a well-run ecological economy would adjust production to needs, which can surely be done democratically, rather than by authoritative methods. But these desirable methods or policies will not increase employment, merely keep it nicely steady. Therefore the wealth-increasing strategies will be essential.

To summarize, an ecological economy would look always at needs:

> The need for better infrastructure
>
> The need to restore and/or improve the commons
>
> The need to preserve biodiversity
>
> The need for better, largely organic farming
>
> The need to restore and/or improve forest
>
> The need for improved education.

Feel free to add to this list.

At first, the wealth-increasing measures will easily bring about full employment, since the commons have been neglected for centuries. But eventually an equilibrium may be reached at which all of the above, production, services and the rest will not quite maintain full employment. Should that happen, then reduced working hours must be considered. This is nothing new [3].

To conclude, the above is the basis for full employment in developed countries and those with plentiful natural resources. For countries with little in the way of natural resources, investment in green technology will prove beneficial in the long term, but generous support from richer countries may be necessary for the investment, which should be set in a framework that leads to sustainability, not dependency. Setting up the ecological economy in the majority of now-prosperous countries will assist in the further necessary steps, as these become clearer.

Notes

1. *Le Devoir*, 18 January 2017, pp. A1 and A8.

2. Increasing built capital is most often desirable, though it can give rise to conflict within the wider world of all species, when it destroys or infringes upon habitat. Because the human race has so extremely expanded its numbers, the question of infringement on habitat of other species is ever present in developed countries and those with high population densities.

3. An early book on the subject of greatly reduced working hours was W H Lever's *The Six Hour Day and Other Industrial Questions* London: George, Allen and Unwin (1918).

Chapter Eight

Putting an End to Fossil-Fuel Burning

It is urgent, very urgent that the human race stop burning fossil fuels. Continuance of this bad habit will guarantee a change in climate type, and we are uncomfortably close to the tipping point beyond which the climate change will continue on its path by virtue of the feedbacks alone (see Appendix 1). Furthermore, the transition has already progressed so far that much of the CO_2 already added to the atmosphere will have to be reabsorbed, a huge undertaking; and the amount to be reabsorbed is increasing at its maximum rate because the emissions themselves are still increasing. The sooner significant reductions take place, the less carbon dioxide will diffuse into the ocean, and this is most important. Sequestering CO_2 that is already in the atmosphere is likely to prove a huge challenge and costly in human effort and resources [1]. For the above reasons, it should begin without delay.

Where the required technologies already exist, major steps toward eliminating greenhouse gas (ghg) emissions can be achieved in little over twenty years. In the United States, a task of closing the many coal-burning power stations must be faced, but the technology to do that also exists, thanks to the low price now achievable with photovoltaic systems. This leaves the matter of supplying the baseload (the minimum power needed at night), for which a combination of water, wind and nuclear power are available [2]. Reducing the baseload is a valuable strategy for dealing with night-time electrical supply, and it is surprising that it has not been more widely adopted, since *conservation* has long been a buzz word among activists for a sustainable planet as well as those responsible for energy supply and distribution.

Priorities

Recently, a new modeling tool, the Canadian Energy Systems Simulator (CanESS), has emerged from Robert Hoffman's group in Ottawa that produced the global economic model GSS, referred to earlier [3]. CanESS was designed to assist governments, provincial or federal, to choose policies that would enable the elimination of ghg emissions to be realized *in a minimum time*. Doubtless the CanESS, or a very similar tool tailored to the needs of another region, could be used elsewhere to equal advantage.

Inevitably, such a tool can also be used to arrive at policies that would achieve the elimination of ghg emissions at the lowest financial cost. This alternative, as Hoffman himself emphasizes, goes against the intention behind the CanESS, since we are here dealing with a global crisis, in which monetary cost must be a secondary consideration. I am reminded of the words of the late John Hotson, economist, who said, "Could anything be more insane than for the human race to die out because we 'couldn't afford' to save ourselves?"

Since the CanESS is in its early stages of use, Hoffman has himself been experimenting with it (private communication, June 2016) and has come up with and later confirmed the following very significant preliminary conclusions:

> **The standard negotiating routes for the reductions of ghg emissions, namely carbon taxes or cap and trade, will not produce the final result of zero emissions soon enough to meet Nature's deadline;**

> **Governmental policies are urgently needed 1) to convert all electrical production to non-emitting methods and 2) to eliminate emissions from all surface transportation.**

Hoffman selected the above policies, 1) and 2), because the needed technologies already exist. It is simply a matter of implementing them, and making sure that private industry collaborates in doing this. The manufacturers of trucks, vans and cars would have to prepare to sell only non-emitting vehicles by a certain date, not many years from now. Hoffman believes that emissions-free electrical generation and transport could be achieved in Ontario by the year 2040 and I support his view. In Quebec and elsewhere, such a result could also be achieved in the same time period. But it will require a firm policy in each such case.

The working of an economic market under carbon taxes or cap and trade would be too slow. It is easy to extend this type of reasoning for planning throughout North America and beyond.

Movement in the above sectors would encourage a new focus on reducing the emissions of the other sectors in the economy.

The above is not an argument against a carbon tax, but merely a statement that such a tool will not suffice, because we humans have left it too late for a carbon tax to do its work. Firm decisions are now essential to accomplish what can be accomplished by the earliest practicable dates.

Cost, in the parlance of an ecological economy, amounts to the resources and person-hours that are required to accomplish the task. The money merely serves the purpose of distribution of those resources and their functioning to achieve the desired, vital task. This is a very different attitude to money than one ever hears in the traditional economy, but will be predominant in an ecological economy. Should we even be worried about money? Few people have raised hackles about the more than trillion dollars spent annually on military production and on the maintenance of armed forces, and most of such expenditures end up causing death and destruction or end up as waste. The ecological economy will use resources to counter climate change and to increase wealth, the opposite of what military production and activities do.

With regard to major projects necessarily involving the creation of large sums of money, it may be necessary, occasionally or constantly, to have anti-inflation policies in place. Full employment does not have to be accompanied by inflation.

The later stages of reduction of ghg emissions

There is no reason to delay efforts in the other sectors of the economy, where elimination of emissions may be more difficult. The sooner the necessary research and development is achieved the better, as the emissions in these sectors must also be brought to zero. A sector where work could begin at once, and where emissions are particularly high is production of cement for making concrete. The emissions are due to

a) burning fossil fuel to heat the calcium carbonate, which is the raw material for cement, and b) the CO_2 emitted from the carbonate during the heating. The heating could in principle be electrical, whereas the emissions from the heated carbonate are inevitable and consist of CO_2, which is in this case free of the other bi-products of combustion in air. The problem then becomes how and where to store the CO_2 permanently. Or can it be used for something? A potential use of CO_2 lies in the production of algae, on which much research has been done these last decades [4]. Changing the manufacture of concrete to the point it is non-emitting would normally be tested in a pilot plant before going to full scale. There is, in addition, the possibility of the manufacture of a new type of concrete, not based upon calcium oxide, and thus circumventing the emissions that arise from heating the calcium carbonate [5].

It is not too early to ask: do we have competent people assigned to these tasks all of which are urgent? And have any of them been funded to begin their work?

By attending in such ways to every sector of the economy, one can envision a variety of emissions-free countries well within 60 years.

The importance of going forward

The optimum attitude for any nation is surely to reduce its emissions to zero in the shortest time it can, even if some nations lag sadly behind their example. The more rapidly emissions are reduced to zero in any sector of any of the world's economies, the greater the hope of a successful outcome globally; and the more the avant-garde nations achieve in the reductions of emissions, the more useful know-how will be available for nations that lag in this.

The human and technological skills of all nations are needed to lead the way in elimination of ghg emissions, regardless of what some nations may not yet be doing.

This is what will produce an effect.

Notes

1. Global Carbon Capture and Storage Institute
    https://www.globalccsinstitute.com/
    also
    https://en.wikipedia.org/wiki/Biosequestration
    www.kisstheground.com/Carbon
    In addition, there is a wide range of recent and forthcoming books
    with titles such as *Carbon Capture and Storage*.

2. This author does not favor nuclear energy as a general option, but
    believes that solar concentration using a Fresnel lens instead of
    mirrors, an inert gas working substance such as nitrogen, and storage
    of heat in rocks of just the right size holds promise for latitudes
    within, say, 30 degrees of the equator—see end of chapter Twenty-
    One and footnote 8 in that chapter.

3. The Canadian Energy Systems Simulator is the creation of Robert
    Hoffman, Bert McInnis and collaborators at WhatIf? Technologies
    in Ottawa.

4. Algae of various kinds can be copiously produced by the action
    of sunlight on water containing high concentrations of CO_2. For
    example, edible algae have been produced in this way, and algae from
    which biofuels are being produced.

5. An example of research in this area is T Zhang et al. "Formation
    of magnesium silicate hydrate (M-S-H) pastes using sodium
    hexametaphosphate" *Cement and Concrete Research* **65** pp.8-14
    2014.

Chapter Nine

Minimizing Extraction and Maximizing Re-use and Recycling

This chapter may at first appear as bad news for the mining industry, since an ecological economy must minimize extraction; however, a long-term view will show that the suggested path will in fact extend the mining industry's lifetime of prosperity and extend the possibility of human prosperity. Mining has attracted much negative attention because of the state of mine sites after a mine is closed and because of various forms of pollution resulting from mining processes during and long after mining operations have ceased. The consequences of tar-sands extraction in Alberta are perhaps the worst such on record. A visit to Kirkland Lake (in northern Ontario) in the period 1960-80, where there had once been six active gold mines, may have shocked visitors, as there was no lake. It had been filled in with mining tailings! The tailings, furthermore, were contaminated with cyanide, making them difficult materials to re-use. Another example of pollution arises at uranium mine sites, where the uranium has been separated from the ore at the site and the radium is left among the tailings. Although the gross quantities of radium are small, the fact that radium is hugely more radioactive than uranium renders the tailings toxic, and the radium, furthermore, emits radon, a radioactive gas, which then diffuses into the atmosphere as a radioactive pollutant.

Slowly the mining industry is making progress on most fronts, so that the transition to an ecological economy will not likely be a dramatic explosion of environmental virtue, but a gradual continuance of the present trends, with help from the new paradigm (see Chapter One) and a changing attitude toward increasing natural wealth. Furthermore, there may not be any decrease in mining output in the early stages of an ecological economy, since the poorer countries will continue to be in a process of development, it is to be hoped, toward sustainability.

A key question for the ecological economy is: do the technologies already exist that would make mining satisfactory environmentally? The answer seems to be generally, "yes," and a great deal of progress is being made to implement what can now be implemented. The pressure for such implementation comes from jurisdictions that do not want their environment spoiled, and from the greater profit that can come from forestalling pollution. Regulation is playing a major role. In a fully ecological economy, the mining companies would most likely all be benefit corporations (see Chapter Thirteen), having legal structures that would not require much, if any additional regulation. None of the foregoing implies that there are no longer mining companies that take advantage where there is weak regulation to extract minerals at the lowest overall financial cost, but rather that we are in a state of changing goals, overall good news.

Successfully reclaimed mining sites

According to Cornerstone editors Krutka and Jingfeng, some closed mine sites are now forests, farms, open spaces or public parks [1]. In some countries a permit to mine is not granted unless there is a full closure plan prepared in advance. The costs per site can be high, though the average is estimated at only $1.5 million (USD) [2].

Mining (TZWM)

More good news comes from the announcement of Canadian Government support for clean technology development in mining and other resource industries. Federal funds devoted to the mining sector and matched by that industry will thereby have the opportunity to transform some mining processes, advance energy efficiency and reduce CO_2 emissions [3]. TZWM, involving 40 companies, is a strategy of the Canadian Mining Innovation Council (CMIC).

Keeping track of extracted materials: resource accounting

Julian Ortiz Cabrera writes: ". . . the mining industry still suffers [from] an "extractivism fever," that is, the focus is still in the extraction process rather than in the optimization of the use of the extracted resource. . . in Chile, little effort exists to track the extracted resources to know what is its final use. . . I can see a complete absence of planning regarding the extraction of resources at a country level, that is, the Mining Ministry does not control how much [is] produced, but only cheers for more production . . . I can see a similar behavior in . . . most South American and African countries, and even in Australia.

"Europe has focused on a different goal, which is to ensure the access to raw materials to sustain their development." [4]

Resource accounting is a significant requirement of an ecological economy.

Reduce, re-use and recycle

The title of this section is a catch phrase that refers to the need for reduced use of materials, the need to re-use products that are in principle re-usable, and to recycle the rest. The reduction of material consumption often goes counter to the desire for more by way of standard of living. There are, however, ways of reducing that come with technological breakthroughs. Buying Kindle editions of books is just one example. By contrast, the same kinds of technical advance can bring about more use of resources. For example, the invention of personal computers has caused immense amounts of physical waste, because of rapidly evolving equipment that quickly rendered the earlier types obsolete. There's a connection between quality and reducing material output that tends to be neglected, but is coming into evidence through the longer useful lives of some automobiles.

Re-use is almost equally obvious as a step toward sustainability. Re-used glass bottles require much less energy to clean and return than the manufacture of new ones.

After all the reductions that can be achieved and re-using anything that practicability allows, we still have immense tonnages of useful materials going to landfill, and this is where recycling becomes important.

Many industries, including mining have adopted recycling as an essential component of their operation, something that can be done for profit and give them a good profile in the public's view. See, for example, Annie Leonard's *The Story of Stuff* (Free Press 2010), in which she provides more than a dozen discussions of recycling.

Of particular interest is *extended producer responsibility*, an industrial system originating in Germany whereby producers of goods become financially responsible for the waste arising from packaging that they use. Under this system, producers tend to avoid unnecessary packaging, or packaging that is heavy or involves dangerous materials. In North America, where the extended producer responsibility has not yet been generally adopted, people are being "drowned" in packaging (Annie Leonard's choice of verb), which seems ever to be increasing. Around the year 2000, ballpoint pens were still sold individually and one could test them in shops prior to purchase. Then, about five years later they were all encased in stiff plastic packages. It seemed at that time there was nothing much left to put inside plastic except green vegetables and this has since happened to a considerable extent, with a conspicuous increase in plastic waste! Wrapped goods can also be put inside a second covering of plastic, and Styrofoam became fashionable as an underlay for foods, so the "plastic war" (my expression) continued and is continuing, in opposition to what is needed in an ecological economy.

Because of excessive packaging, frequent lack of re-use and failure to adopt extended producer responsibility, municipal waste is excessive in much of North America, and is surely serious elsewhere; and it falls to the municipalities to dispose of it or recycle it. It has been estimated that between 88 and 96 percent of a city's garbage can be recycled, some as compost, and the rest in the categories: paper, cardboard, glass, metals and plastics. If the compostable materials are duly composted, that leaves the other five categories, which go to landfill in the absence of any recycling. The recycling of any of those five categories is called "diversion," that is, from landfill. In the USA, the city of San Francisco already had achieved 70 percent diversion by 2007-8 and proudly aims for 100 percent (perhaps not quite practicable) but the city already achieved 77 percent by 2010, and continues on the upward path. The city of Toronto in Canada made some progress from 44 percent diversion in 2009, but got stuck at 52 percent diversion over the years 2012-15. Many cities have not even achieved Toronto's 52 percent. Obviously there is far to go.

Summary

Re-use and recycling are essential for a truly ecological economy, and there is an increasing consciousness that these processes are important, more so the larger the population. But it is financial cost that limits the pursuit of these goals in most jurisdictions. The same is true for mining, where there is, however, a prospect of government support for TZWM. By contrast, the ecological economy will reckon resource/capital costings completely instead of only fiscally, and thus greatly accelerate the adoption of maximum re-use and recycling, as well as beneficial programs such as TZWM.

Notes

1. Holly Krutka and Li Jingfeng "Case Studies of Successfully Reclaimed Mining Sites" *Cornerstone* is the official journal of the coal industry http://cornerstonemag.net/case-studies-of-successfully-reclaimed ...

2. Krutka and Jingfeng *loc. cit.* In this case, I am obliged to quote the fiscal cost, whereas in the spirit of ecological economics I would have preferred to give the full costs in natural units.

3. TZMW research and development will include: replacing diesel-powered equipment by electric or renewable; recapturing otherwise lost energy; minimization of waste, treating waste water and tracking water quality in real time; improving ore reserve definition to minimize waste extraction; and reducing various costs.

4. Julian Ortiz Cabrera private communication March 2017. Professor Ortiz Cabrera is a professor at the Mining School, Queens University, Kingston Ontario.

Chapter Ten

Business and Industrial Goals in the New Economy

One of the nice things about a nonviolent change from a traditional economy to one that is fully ecological, is that there may be some things that can simply continue as they are (more or less). This chapter will therefore concentrate mainly on violations of good principle in the traditional economy, where change is essential.

To make a profit in business, one needs customers or clients, and much good is produced in trying to satisfy them and keep them in this state. There are nevertheless several factors enabling corporations to keep their customers and yet do environmental harm, including harm to human health.

This is an area where changing the mindset is particularly important. In the long term what is better for the ecosphere is going to be better for the corporation too.

Environmentally damaging processes

Modern democracies have the immense advantage of nongovernmental groups—often well informed on particular environmental matters—who have challenged and continue to challenge certain industries to do better in their environmental performance. While the effects of such nongovernmental groups have been beneficial, not all enterprises take up the challenges, and serious environmental damage continues. Examples are: mercury pollution arising from paper mills in remote areas; poor handling of radioactive or chemical wastes; inappropriate clear cutting in forests; and oil spills.

The legal instruments for preventing serious environmental damage would appear to be already in place, though not necessarily fully used. When huge environmental damage has been done these last decades, as in a major oil spill, it has tended to result merely in large fines imposed on the offending corporation. Wouldn't the withdrawal of the corporate charter of the offending company be more appropriate? Surely, in such extreme cases, the shareholders should be obliged to restructure the corporation and seek a new charter, or sell their assets. A new board and a new charter, preferably as a benefit corporation (see chapter 13), could set operations on a new and more responsible course.

Human health

Despite tight food safety regulations in prosperous countries, protecting people from dangerous substances in food, the same scrupulous attention has not been accorded to optimizing the benefits of food. Examples are in wheat milling, bread making and the over-use of sugar in processed foods. In 2004, FEASTA published its Review number 2 [1], which contained an article by Frank Rotering, "Putting Human Health Before Profit." Rotering argues that human health and wellbeing are parameters than can be measured objectively, and recommends these as indicators and goals for a "new economy." He was not thinking of a fully ecological economy (was anyone in 2004?), but his criterion was excellent from the standpoint of this chapter. Indeed, the United Nations puts out periodic assessments of how various nations are doing, and human health or wellbeing is always on the list.

In North America, junk food abounds to the point that, if everyone suddenly stopped buying it, there wouldn't be enough of the good, nutritious stuff to go round! We would be forced to eat at least some junk food until the food industry had revised its methods so as to provide for us all really well. As things stand, there is increasing obesity, which the medics agree is a "problem," and a range of other diet-related complaints, but no visible political response from ministers of health. And meanwhile, junk food continues to dominate entire food outlets. More serious and dangerous are the medical effects arising from the use of chemical fertilizers, pesticides and weed killers by agribusiness, and these are touched upon in Chapter Seventeen.

What then about junk food? Aren't people doing rather well in spite of it, and living longer, often much longer than their parents? Yes, they are living longer, but we are far from a maximum in this respect. An experienced physician once said to me that his observation of the human body over many years was that it was designed to last 95 years, by which time the nervous system was coming to the end of its design-life. There's likely some truth in this, but then, what about the centenarians?

In the meantime, the expectation of life is far below the aforesaid physician's best estimate, so there's work to be done: to reduce junk food, attain great reductions in obesity, diabetes, arthritis and many other chronic complaints, and change attitudes so as to encourage meaningful and creative activities long past a conventional retirement age. A change to an ecological economic system would be immensely beneficial in all of the above.

Other aspects of food and human health are discussed in Chapter Seventeen.

Industrial production

This topic is so extensive and complex that this chapter can only skim over it. Annie Leonard provides us with relevant material in chapter 2 on this subject in her book, *The Story of Stuff*, revealing many unhappy truths of industrial production. The emphasis here, however, must be to follow up the benefits of new thinking in the EE. Perhaps some new rules will be called for; but the hope is that actions will follow the new thought patterns, optimizing ecological health.

Packaging

The excesses of packaging in modern business are discussed in Chapter Nine in the section "Reduce, re-use and recycle."

Planned obsolescence

Planned obsolescence is something that shouldn't even exist in any economy, and must surely disappear in the EE.

There are principles of industrial design, whose neglect can give rise to planned obsolescence, and the relevant parts read something like this. A good design is such that the parts will come to the end of their useful life (that is: wear out, cease to function) at about the same time; but if one or more of the parts are bound to wear out sooner, then those must be available as spares and easily replaced. Industries have frequently violated that design principle in the interest of producing some product at low cost, which facilitates its sale in today's competitive market. Unfortunately, this can give rise to products that cannot be repaired, at least, not without the sophisticated equipment of the manufacturer! And the sale of such products, especially at very low prices, encourages such production. In some cases, upon receiving a complaint from a customer, the retailer simply replaces the damaged article, and sends the damaged goods to landfill; in others, the purchaser simply takes the loss, likewise putting the damaged goods in the bin that goes to landfill. The manufacturers know what features doom a product to landfill. This is the crux of planned obsolescence, coupled to the fact that low-cost items that have traveled an ocean prior to their sale are in any case not going to be shipped back to the plant of origin. Today's problem doesn't resemble yester year's and is doubtless closely related to the globalization of trade, with its increasing transport across the ocean. Planned obsolescence can surely be reduced more easily under conditions of local production (see next chapter).

Deliberate destruction of new produce

The deliberate destruction of goods is not often reported. There were cases in the 1930s when loads of ripe tomatoes were dumped into Lake Erie. This occurred in the depression, when many people were poor to the point of hunger. A recent example of destruction of goods in North America was reported for unsold clothes that could in principle have been exported to wherever they might be needed [2].

A controversial example of destruction arose in California following General Motor's scrapping recently developed electric cars [3]. The cars had been rented out to customers since 1996 but were scrapped in 2002.

Notes

1. FEASTA Review number 2 *Growth: The Celtic Cancer* 2004. FEASTA is the acronym for the Foundation for the Economics of Sustainability.

2. *Le Devoir* (Montreal) 30 December 2016, A3: "(translating) . . . unsold [clothes] were destroyed and put in the garbage."

3. Wikipedia "General Motors EV1"

Chapter Eleven

Local Production and Trade

Globalization is already here, and we can see it all around us. Products that used to be considered foreign can be bought almost anywhere. Name your favorite motor vehicle. Is there anywhere you are likely to live where it would not be available or it couldn't be serviced? Consider food for a moment. What are the fruits that grow near where you live? Are these the only ones available in the food stores you visit? Unlikely! And what about vacations? Have you noticed the number of choices offered? Or the number of people wanting holidays abroad? Evidently people like to have such choices, and few would give them up willingly.

A useful basis for continuing this discussion is Richard Douthwaite's article, "Why localization is essential for sustainability" [1]. Part of his thesis claims that the globalized economy is unsustainable, and furthermore contains a positive feedback that renders it more so. Enter climate change and the fact that we must stop putting greenhouse gases into the atmosphere. How are we going to continue air travel at its present scale, let alone its increases? And how are we going to enable more and more container ships to sail the ocean?

The greenhouse gas emissions from such transport are significant, though the fuels for air and sea transport are barely taxed. For shipping, the tax rates are different in different jurisdictions, but everywhere the tax rate is very low relative to what it would have to be to discourage burning that fuel. The tax therefore has nothing to do with addressing climate change. Yet, even at the insignificant levels of the tax from a climate standpoint, the small differences of tax level between one jurisdiction and another are sufficient to affect operators of airlines or shipping because of the intensity of competition in the global market!

Evidently, the determination to continue and increase international trade and tourism are proceeding entirely without regard to the necessity to reduce ghg emissions—a thorny unsolved problem for modern trade in the climate change context.

Let us look for a moment at Douthwaite's conclusions on what to do about globalization, in the framework of needing a sustainable civilization. Reverting completely to local production, though perhaps possible in principle, is unthinkably difficult, and brings with it the negative factor that certain types of production, automobiles for example, need to exploit economies of scale; otherwise production becomes too inefficient. Douthwaite therefore favors the plausible alternative, namely to localize production where it makes any sense to do so, but to leave the major stuff requiring economies of scale globalized. This second choice he accompanies with much advice, such as the disadvantages of local economies taking loans from outside their currency area; here it is noteworthy that in the ecological economy outlined in this book there would be no need for such loans. Nevertheless, the re-institution of local production everywhere with the aforementioned exceptions presents a formidable challenge, though it would turn out a satisfying one, and economically stable, if the politicians are willing to leave it so.

What does this mean, in practical terms? It would mean eating mainly foods that have been grown locally, and wearing clothes that had mostly been produced locally, etc. And of course there could be occasional exceptions. The system worked well, for example in the 1950s, except for inadequacies arising from the traditional economic system itself, and it can be made to work in the new economy, with the advantages of what has been learned about production since then.

Like Douthwaite, I had not been able to see an alternative to leaving many portions of international trade globalized, though I have often questioned in my own mind the huge extent of such trade and of tourism.

Above all, we must face up to the problem of ghg emissions. For both air and ocean transport, a long-term future cannot be based upon fossil fuels. The first and greatest single step toward sustainability is the reduction to zero everywhere of greenhouse gas emissions from those fuels. This alone, according to the global footprint layer-cake diagram, could bring the world's footprint down to about 1.0, the upper limit for global sustainability [2].

For long-term air and ocean travel it leaves only one plausible solution, and that is the non-polluting combination of fuels: oxygen and hydrogen, both of which must be stored as very cold liquids aboard the vessels they propel; in both cases, wind can be an additional propellant, as is very often the case today for jet aircraft in a "jet stream" at high altitude. The oxygen-hydrogen fuel combination has the added advantages of producing no oxides of nitrogen during combustion, and of producing very high burning temperatures, leading to maximum thermal efficiencies in propulsion [3]. Then why, you ask, have such systems not already been put into general use? The standard reply is always "cost." This is the supreme example of inadequate evaluation of cost in the traditional economy. It omits, as modern business mostly does, the huge cost of putting yet more CO_2 and other oxides into the atmosphere, thus acidifying the ocean. I could, of course give you an estimated environmental cost of, say, $1,000 per tonne of liquid fuel of the types used today, but it would be meaningless, since all estimates of this sort have uncertainties, and the uncertainty in the sense "plus" is infinite if use of that fuel might destroy life on Earth. Therefore, though engineering systems of propulsion based upon oxygen and hydrogen might present many challenges, technically successful results are bound to cost less in real ecological terms than what we have now.

Note

1. In *Growth: The Celtic Cancer* "FEASTA Review number 2" ed. Richard Douthwaite and Jon Jopling 2004 pp. 114-23.

2. www.footprintnetwork.org/resources

3. See also Appendix 3 for instructions how to find the layer-cake diagram online.

4. In cases where the high temperature of hydrogen combustion with oxygen would present technical difficulties, the oxygen could easily be diluted with argon.

Chapter Twelve

Advertising and Consumerism

Very many people seem to dislike advertising, yet it is both essential to commerce and completely legitimate in a fundamental way. Businesses need to advertise what they have to offer, a factor older than the banking system. The problem is in the details. Some authors have revealed their dislikes as arising from ads spoiling their view of things. They don't like placards in public places, especially where they obstruct the view of some splendid architecture, or of verdant countryside. Others don't like having films on TV, or broadcast concerts or plays interrupted by a "commercial." They believe that a time sequence should not be interrupted in that way. Others dislike the intrusion of commerce into their private space, and advertising can surely be an intrusion. Yet others dislike commercial activity on days that they consider sacred, or times of rest.

And all these views have validity, but none of them is objective in the sense that everyone would be in agreement with abolishing intrusive advertising or commercial placards. And besides, some say of the media, "How would you pay for the things you watch on television or hear on radio if it weren't for advertising?" And that too is a valid question.

The above introduction is far too brief, since advertising has a major new, ever-dynamic field on the internet, which I cannot begin to discuss here. Rather, I hope merely to introduce the notion that advertising had already established important goals and methods prior even to the invention of the internet, and that new departures from the onset of the internet, are extensions and complications made possible by the new technology, and the speed of transmitting its messages.

What then needs to be addressed here and now?

And that does have an answer, since advertising has made a major contribution in establishing overconsumption, a serious factor in creating the society of waste, and the high global footprint of today's world. It has not been alone in this, but here let's simply look at what must change in advertising if a sustainable world is ever to be achieved.

The advertising industry has been systematic in developing methods of inducing people, through their ads, to want to own things or buy things that they do not need, or how to improve upon what they already have. The incessant message is that this product (whatever) is essential to you or that you cannot really live without it, or that your happiness depends on having it. Juliet Schor has written extensively on this subject and can testify to a relatively new addiction of humans, namely the addiction to shopping. Her descriptions of waste are graphic.

But it gets worse. The psychological craft of advertising can also persuade you to purchase products that are not good for health. Cigarettes are just one obvious example, but there follows a panoply of food products, mainly processed foods, that are less than good or far from optimal. Let's call it the junk food industry, not intending to mean that any given item is poisonous, merely that it doesn't contribute to nourishment in the needed diversity and proportions for human diet. All these foods are advertised, else they will drop in popularity and their producers will lose income. Much research and development went into many of these products, and the manufacturers then need to profit from them. And I daresay most of these products are completely harmless if taken rather occasionally, and taken by young people in great health. But, taken often or consistently by people of all ages, some of those products can prove very harmful in the long run.

Remedial action against the practices and trends indicated above would seem essential for a sustainable economy, most especially during the many years starting now during which the human race must direct its attention cooperatively to prevent a climate transition. Health will be vitally important.

I present no answers in this area, and ask readers to come up with their own ideas, for public debate.

But I will risk an umbrella proposal: that changes in advertising should be planned so as to place a strong emphasis on health. May 6, 2014, MacLeans Magazine published an entire issue on sugar, with the heading writ large on the cover: *Death by Sugar*. The issue spelled out in detail the various ways in which the food industry slowly kills some people through an excessive use of sugar, supplied in small or large amounts in most processed foods (including drinks). I subsequently read the labels on all salad dressings offered at a supermarket, and was surprised to find they all contained sugar. The health effects of sugar make it undesirable in such products; and its ubiquitous use make the scale of its effects deadly.

My second umbrella suggestion would be that advertising companies in future be registered as benefit corporations (see Chapter Thirteen), so that their charters would respect the need for optimum human health and environmental sustainability. This then raises the question of what to do about advertising companies that already have their license to practice their arts.

If it seems early in the day for such proposals, it is surely time to begin the search for a way forward.

Bibliography

Naomi Oreskes *Merchants of Doubt: How a Handful of Scientists Obscured the truth on a Handful of Issues from Tobacco Smoke to Global Warming* 2011.

Juliet B Schor *The Overspent American: Upscaling, Downshifting and the new Consumer* 1996.

Juliet B Schor *Born to Buy: The Commercialized Child and the New Consumer Culture* 2005.

Chapter Thirteen

Encouragement of Benefit Corporations

A benefit corporation is one whose corporate charter includes goals that are beneficial to humanity and/or the environment in addition to the goal of profit-making. In this way the benefit corporation differs very distinctly from traditional corporations, which legally have only the responsibility to make profit. Corporations can be and are subjected to regulations, which force them to maintain certain environmental or other standards, but the benefit corporation would in principle conform of itself with a regulation its charter already required.

To establish benefit corporations in any given jurisdiction requires new legislation. The idea took root first in Maryland, which became the first state, not only in the USA but in the world, to pass the required legislation [1]. This historic event, which passed unnoticed by most people, opened a new channel of hope in the development of future industry and businesses, since the benefit corporation will of itself conduct its business in accord with the environmental and social needs of the world community, as expressed in its charter.

The Maryland legislation came into effect in October 2010, to be followed by New Jersey and Hawaii, Vermont and Virginia in 2011, California, New York, Washington, South Carolina, Louisiana and Massachusetts in 2012, Illinois, Pennsylvania, Washington DC, Arkansas, Delaware in 2013; and the number has now passed thirty states.

In general, the purposes of a benefit corporation include that it

* shall create public benefit, and

* shall have the right to name specific public benefit purposes.

The registration of new benefit corporations in jurisdictions that have passed the necessary law is therefore of great interest in development toward a sustainable economy worldwide.

The spread of analogous legislation to other jurisdictions is also looming, and much to be encouraged. On 22 December 2015, Italy's government approved a Benefit Corporation law, making Italy the first government outside the United States to take this step [2]. A benefit corporation in Italy will be known as *una Società Benefit*.

Changes to Australia's Corporations Act are being drafted to create "benefit corporations"—a new form of for-profit for-purpose business—that will be put to government later in 2017 [3].

Overall, these rapid legal developments seem to be going ahead, in keeping with public and environmental needs. This would appear to be one of the most encouraging indicators of a move toward an ecological economy.

In August 2014, the Canadian Bar Association "urged that Parliament change the federal statute under which businesses are established to make it clear that corporations can pursue public benefit purposes beyond pure profit [4]."

B corporations

The expression *B-corporation* is confusing because it can be an abbreviation for *benefit corporation,* but more properly means a corporation that has been certified as having maintained certain environmental standards [5]. The difference is very significant, because B-corporations are certified corporations that have the usual legal basis requiring their directors only to make profit for their shareholders, and may only be conforming with given environmental standards for the sake of reputation.

Notes

1. http://www.futurepolicy.org/business-priorities/maryland-benefit-corporations/

2. http://bcorporation.eu/blog/italian-parliament-approves-benefit-corporation-legal-status

3. Probonoaustralia.com.au 9 March 2016.

Chapter Fourteen

Banking Requirements

Chapter Four Introduced the general notion that in moving to an ecological economy it will be necessary to choose a banking system to match the economy. One type of solution would essentially separate the task of generating funds for ecological progress from the existing banking system, and it would do this by creating new, publicly owned banks to issue the required funds at zero interest.

This choice would circumvent the problems of reforming the present banking system at the outset, though it would necessitate the adoption of controls where very large sums had to be generated.

Others may argue that it would be more appropriate to redesign the entire banking system at the outset, constructing it so that it can handle the measures needed to address climate change and finance ecologically important projects.

The above debate cannot be settled here.

In either case, publicly owned banks are relevant. According to Ellen Hodgson Brown, in her book *The Public Bank Solution* (2013), 45 percent of banks are publicly owned in Brazil, 60 percent in Russia, 75 percent in India and 69 percent in China. She calls these the BRIC countries. The four countries together have 41 percent of the global population, a very significant fraction of publicly owned banks, and go-ahead economies. One needs to ask whether they have already made a significant breakthrough on the way to fully ecological economies. This question is too large to handle in this book, but Chapter Twenty-One gives a partial answer for the world's most populous country and largest economy, China.

A global ecological economy that can address climate change needs an adequate number and distribution of sources of interest-free money. The United States and Europe have large economies spanning extended territories, while Canada, with its much smaller population, has the world's second-largest territory. These three areas, together with the BRIC countries have more than half the world's population and the world's two largest economies (as measured by gross domestic product). It would seem that the USA and Europe must stand at a great disadvantage among the BRIC countries if they do not have public banks. Canada has a public bank, the Bank of Canada, but doesn't use it to crate interest-free money, because of an agreement under the rules of the Bank of International Settlements (BIS). Obviously, some rules must be changed.

The European Union and the USA have different histories, but both of these large agglomerations of states were brought together without due attention to redistribution of wealth. Full employment gives rise in a natural way to a degree of redistribution since the poorer areas of a large country are often plagued with high unemployment. Full employment, however, requires the aforesaid new banks, as well as the programs they will fund.

As stated briefly in Chapter Four, the Bank of Canada was used to fund Canada's part in WWII very fully, and there were no unfortunate economic consequences, because the debt burden was very small. By contrast, the federal governments of both Canada and the United States have huge national debts today, with preposterous debt burdens, and some Canadian provinces are heavily indebted. Evidently the chosen forms of economy and banking systems haven't suited these countries very well.

It is significant too that Canada's funding policy at the outset of WWII provided full employment, when there had been considerable unemployment right up to the outbreak of war. The system of financing used by Prime Minister Mackenzie King served to face the emergency as then perceived. Today the emergency may be less obvious, but it is much more deeply threatening. Surely this is not the time to delay, but to act in the interest of all.

I therefore propose, for all small single-currency areas, that publicly-owned banks be created where none exist, together with a watch-dog economic committee to prevent great excesses of money in circulation through appropriate action.

For large, single-currency areas, it may be necessary to choose among several routes. The first would be a series of regional banks set up for wealth creation, with a linking mechanism that would prevent any one from drowning the country in new money and thus inhibit other regions from legitimate wealth-creating activities. Another would be to do it through parallel currencies. This also would be a complex process, because some wealth-creating strategies might span several regions, while others might be very local. A compromise of the following kind might work: a national or central, publicly-owned bank to deal with the larger, more widespread programs, while the new regional banks would issue currency (and/or parallel currency) for more local projects.

For the United States and for Europe, to have private, for-profit banks as their central banks must surely be untenable in the present circumstances.

One of the problems of determining a fiscal future is that today's experts are ALL traditional economists or financiers. There aren't any experts in ecological economics. There are people who have written books about aspects of an ecological economy, but they cannot be expert, because we don't have such an economy to be expert in! The question of staffing the new institutions is therefore tricky. It will require people with the new mindset, even if a few of the wise older heads are necessary.

Old institutions such as the International Monetary Fund (IMF) will have to be set aside, since their basis and philosophy are set in the crumbling concrete of neoliberalism. Giving the IMF responsibility for Greece during its financial crisis made this very evident.

Many people of wonderful good will have contributed generously and intelligently to the work of the World Bank. The founding financial basis of that well-meaning institution is, however, such that it cannot succeed in its mission. It is financially tied to Wall Street, and must therefore work on outdated financial principles, which were never good in the first place.

Parallel currencies

A parallel currency is one that is created and used in a single-currency area that already has its own, government-approved currency. Most parallel currencies have been designed to assist in providing people with needed spending money in hard times or with additional spending money in not-so-bad times. For example, a parallel currency could have helped Ireland out of its fiscal difficulties within the European Union. In such a case, the parallel currency would have a fixed trading value relative to the Euro and would be official, legal tender within the whole country, but could not be used abroad. A currency parallel to the national currency complicates banking because either one must add accounts in the parallel currency, or the existing accounts must be changed to cope with both currencies.

The foregoing illustrates a method of putting more money into circulation without impairing the value of an internationally exchanged currency. A parallel currency could thus be useful for wealth creation in a region of a large single-currency area.

Most parallel currencies today are not, however, national but local, and unofficial.

Two examples of local parallel currencies

A local parallel currency was set up in the town or Wörgl, Austria, in the period 1932-33, a time of severe economic depression. The objective was to raise local prosperity and to do it by issuing new money in the form of municipal certificates having the property suggested much earlier by Sylvio Gesell that there be a charge on money in order to speed its circulation and discourage hoarding. Wörgl achieved this by charging one percent on unspent certificates at the end of each month. The municipality issued these certificates free of charge for projects and local trading purposes, which created jobs, and the certificates were guaranteed by them, indicating the municipality must have had adequate credit in the official currency. The results were: increased prosperity, with the certificates circulating 22 times as fast as regular money; the town reduced its unemployment by 25 percent during the year, and the municipality received 12 percent from the monthly charge on issued certificates. But the National Bank stopped the system, as it went against their monopoly on issuance of new money.

In a more flexible age, a deal could easily be worked out whereby the National Bank could earn part or all of the monthly fee on the unspent certificates, and could thus strike an agreement with a town that wished to put such a system into operation.

It is clear from the Wörgl experience that such a system needs to be officially recognized if it is to avoid the suppression experienced in Wörgl. The strong tendency toward rapid spending in Wörgl's system might tend to exacerbate consumerism in an age such as ours, but it illustrates a system that discourages hoarding of currency, since hoarded currency, while in principle in circulation, is in fact not actually circulating.

A very different system, not requiring a local government initiative, was invented by Michael Linton in 1983 for the community in Courtenay, British Columbia, which was stricken by unemployment at the time. This Local Exchange Trading System (LETS) featured its own currency that was equivalent to the official currency. Trades involving LETS dollars were recorded by a volunteer through communication by telephone. Membership of the LETS system was free, and it was not necessary to open one's LETS account with a deposit; it could equally be opened with a debit. There was no reward for a credit balance nor interest payable on debits. A reason for the relative success of the system was its flexibility, since any trade could be carried out using both the official and LETS currencies. The traders agree on the price, and also on how much of that price would be paid in LETS. An item or service for sale might be paid for 100 percent in LETS currency or any lower percentage. Only the LETS transfers were recorded. The system brought increased prosperity in Courtenay, and was soon copied, often with variants on how it is operated. Today there are hundreds of LETS-type trading groups in many different countries, mainly in Europe, Africa, South America and Australia, often with local names, other than "LETS." The Australian Government has supported LETS in several ways.

Proponents of LETS claim there is no intention to deprive government of tax, and LETS members are encouraged to conform with tax regulations.

Bibliography

Margrit Kennedy *Interest and Inflation Free Money* New Society Publishers 1995.

https://en.wikipedia.org/wiki/Local_exchange_trading_system

Chapter Fifteen

Defining and Restoring the Commons

The expression *the commons* may be less familiar to young people today than it was to their parents or grandparents. In England of the Middle Ages, the expression was widely understood, since there were common grazing lands, and land that was cultivated in common by serfs, people who were not paid but shared in the wealth of the harvest. During my own lifetime, there was still much common grazing on the British moorlands, for example in Yorkshire and in Scotland including the Island of Lewis, off Scotland's northwest coast, and it is likely unchanged. The commons were all over the open land, except where someone had legally obtained exclusive rights to some property or other.

Thus, the commons are intertwined with the law and, in this age of increasing interdependence, legal agreements must sometimes be made to define certain internationally shared commons and strike a deal on how such commons should be respected or maintained. The legal department of the United Nations Environment Program (UNEP) has this to say, by way of definition: "The 'Global Commons' refers to resource domains or areas that lie outside of the political reach of any one nation state." It then identifies the four global commons: the High Seas; the Atmosphere; Antarctica; and, Outer Space. Perhaps the ocean bed deserves separate mention in this list.

The discussion here, however, must go much further than that, to include commons in every land, even if no other state currently has the prospects of rights there. But surely such transnational rights already exist in plenty, because of investment arrangements or treaties, since a corporation may purchase land in another country, if so permitted either by such a treaty or special arrangement. It then matters very much what the buyer does with that land, which can range from land restoration or improvement to pollution or other ruination. The same applies to a buyer already a national of that territory.

For the purposes of this chapter, therefore, I shall adopt the widest possible interpretation of *commons*, to include not only the global commons as defined by UNEP. Any land or water that under the customs of aboriginal peoples would have been shared in common, not across a continent, but throughout a tribal area. A continent was therefore at one time a patchwork of commons. In this way, we shall include waterways, lakes and every type of territory. My proposal therefore harks back to the unwritten but well understood conventions of aboriginal peoples in the Americas, and these have the huge advantage of respect for the land and waterways, exactly what is needed by humanity at large, now that its numbers have overflowed the basket. A new relationship with aboriginal peoples will help realize such goals [1]. The rest will lie in the details. It takes little space to enumerate the possibilities.

> Farmland can be rendered more fertile by the addition of mulch and biochar. This applies to good land that was allowed through dubious farm or forestry practices to deteriorate, or to land that never was fertile. There is a brief discussion of biochar in Appendix 4.

> Waterways can be cleaned up, with measures to prevent unwanted chemicals from entering into the water. If waterways are clean, the lakes or ocean they flow into will eventually be clean.

> Air can be rid of excess carbon dioxide by reducing emissions from fossil fuels and by removal of atmospheric carbon dioxide. The cessation of burning fossil fuels will also have the beneficial effect of eliminating most oxides of nitrogen.

> Species can be preserved through judicious attention to habitat. Various new measures can be adopted to eliminate the unnecessary deaths of birds.

> The sea bed can be protected from trawling and the ocean can be protected from other indiscriminate overfishing.

> Intense irradiation of the ionosphere with electromagnetic radiation for the purposes of military developments can be halted forthwith.

Much more attention can be given to the elimination of contamination of outer space, with special efforts not to contaminate it further.

In an ecological economy, all of these can be attended to, and it is vital that they not be neglected. The profit in all these cases is long-term.

Managing a Commons

So far we have looked at what might need improving in the commons, but no word on management. No chapter even mentioning the commons should omit mention of Elinor Ostrom, who shared the 2009 Swedish National Bank's Prize in Memory of Alfred Nobel. Her first book, on governing the commons, 1990, received its 29th printing in 2011, while her last book, 2007, co-edited with Charlotte Hess, gives us "eight principles for managing a commons" on page 8. See Bibliography.

When it comes to detailed studies on such management, one finds that the work is generally local, and different in detail from place to place. One would thus require a major volume to explain all the workings globally. For this reason, I go no further here than to supply some bibliography.

Afterword

Because of climate change and the huge global population, it follows that growth of trees and plant life is more essential than ever, and it follows from this that any new farm or forest land or green space that is built upon, no matter whether for roads, buildings or parking lots has a negative effect on the commons, and therefore on the ecological balance of the entire world.

Note

1. The work of the Commission on Truth and Reconciliation in Canada and its Calls to Action (2015) form a start to this very necessary process.

Bibliography

Ostrom, Elinor (1990) *Governing the Commons: The Evolution of Institutions for Collective Action* UK Cambridge University Press ISBN 9780521405997.

Ostrom, Elinor and Charlotte Hess eds. (2007) *Understanding knowledge as a commons: from theory to practice* Cambridge Massachusetts MIT Press ISBN 9780262516037.

Chapter Sixteen

The Thorny Problem of Population

The subject of population is so controversial that, even if I try to keep it strictly factual, my conclusions will amount to a point of view. The basic fact to be faced is that the human race, like any other animal species, tends to increase its numbers according to the availability of food, and suffer starvation when the food runs out. The dramatic increases in human population have been due to the invention of farming and subsequent "improvements" in how farming is done, coupled to improved sanitation in cities (drains) and "improvements" in medicine that allow people to live longer [1].

In Britain, where the population has been rising at an average rate of 0.4 percent annually since 1950, some readers might regard the increase insignificant. But this could be a serious error. Any positive rate of rise can produce an unsustainable population if it continues indefinitely.

Britain thus serves as a useful example; it already needed to import much of its food in the early 1950s. Since then its large population density and low and decreasing biocapacity indicate its economy far from sustainable [2]. Britain has nevertheless maintained a sufficient level of prosperity since WWII through exporting manufactured goods, maintaining itself an important financial centre, through tourism and, latterly, the exploitation of North Sea oil, this last being a dubious and transitory benefit. A current projection of its population stated it was headed for 70 million in the year 2050! A long-term population *target* might better be set at 25 million, to match its declining biocapacity more closely.

I've taken Britain as an opening example of failure to face population realities, since that country has a level of education and sophistication of its population that is high in the scheme of world affairs, and it is an island society, though not in any way isolated. And yet the sustainability factor does not seem to have entered into its social planning. Jared Diamond, in his book *Collapse*, describes an isolated island society that survived 3000 years, through limiting its population to what the island could sustain [3]. By contrast Easter Island failed to do this and that society collapsed.

Human history would suggest that, on the continents, an awareness of needing to limit population never developed as had been necessary in isolated islands, because one could invade neighbors to acquire more territory. This type of action must have begun in the fifth millennium BC [4].

In many other areas of the world, especially Africa, this absence of awareness of the need to limit population has surely been revealed, since the populations of some countries have increased by a factor of five in seventy years.

The global population projection in Appendix 2 would suggest the need to halt the current expansion as soon as possible at the lowest possible level: let's say at eight billion. In this way the human race might be spared the appalling threat of population contraction by starvation within thirty years. The problem of feeding more than eight billion people might of course be overcome, but model projections of human population must include the agricultural factors, which UN population projections evidently have omitted. Even the best population projections become increasingly uncertain the further one departs from the present. Today's global population will likely follow the projections discussed in Appendix 2 until a food crisis occurs, or until drought raises its ugly head. And the drought problem is a major international preoccupation as I write.

There is another sufficient reason to halt the population expansion as soon as possible and to begin to decrease human numbers. The human expansion has already crushed the populations of other creatures, most of which are suffering from declines of their habitats, or other depredations that have human cause. Thus, even if our food production can continue at the present level and then increase to meet human needs 30 years from now, countless species will soon become extinct, and most of the rest will be threatened with extinction.

> The new paradigm calling for life-centred economics therefore demands not merely a halt to human population growth, but a decline.

If we are to survive, the ecosphere must survive, and we are killing it, first by putting carbon dioxide into the ocean (via the air) and second, by making it impossible for the world's interdependent species to flourish, in stark violation of what I have sometimes called "The Principle of Life," central to the new paradigm (see Chapter One). Some evidence for the desperate situation of other species is given in Appendix 5.

It is therefore essential to limit the global population very soon, which I believe is possible, and to encourage its slow decline. Evidence for a realistic possibility of an early population maximum was presented at an international roundtable organized by two of my colleagues in 2009 [5]. A speaker on population pointed out that, while the global population had risen by a colossal 75 million souls in 2008, an estimated 80 million pregnancies that same year had been unwanted by the women concerned. Had those women had a choice, there would already have been population stability.

Policy leading to a stable or reducing world population

The preparation of a strategy to attain a stable or diminishing world population has largely been the work of very many women, who came together four times between 1975 and 95 to discuss women's issues, and have continued to this day [6]. In addition, the United Nations sponsored a Conference in Cairo in 1994 [7], which crystallized the key points in a policy to restrain population growth. The conference released its four key points in these terms:

1. **Universal education**: Universal primary education in all countries by 2015. Urge countries to provide wider access for women to secondary and higher level education as well as vocational and technical training.

2. **Reduction of infant and child mortality**: Countries should strive to reduce infant and under-5 child mortality rates by one-third or to 50-70 deaths per 1000 by the year 2000. By 2015 all

countries should aim to achieve a rate below 35 per 1,000 live births and under-five mortality rate below 45 per 1,000.

3. **Reduction of maternal mortality**: A reduction by half the 1990 levels by 2000 and half of that by 2015. Disparities in maternal mortality within countries and between geographical regions, socio-economic and ethnic groups should be narrowed.

4. **Access to reproductive and sexual health services including family planning**: Family-planning counseling, pre-natal care, safe delivery and post-natal care, prevention and appropriate treatment of infertility, prevention of abortion and the management of the consequences of abortion, treatment of reproductive tract infections, sexually transmitted diseases and other reproductive health conditions; and education, counseling, as appropriate, on human sexuality, reproductive health and responsible parenthood. Services regarding HIV/AIDS, breast cancer, infertility, and delivery should be made available. Active discouragement of female genital mutilation (FGM).

It is important to recognize that all four points in the published strategy are essential. Item 1 is essential, since in poor countries not all the children in a family have the opportunity of education beyond the earliest grades. Often it is the girls who are deprived of further education and never complete school. They are thus confined to tasks at home and tend to be married early and start a new family. Education enables them to seek work and postpone marriage until later, an important factor in population growth.

The reduction of child mortality is vital. Frequent infant deaths have always been a motive for wanting many children, since otherwise it was too likely that none would survive to adulthood. This applied in distant times within societies that today are prosperous and now have low birth rates and negligible infant mortality.

The requirement of reduced maternal mortality is an indicator of the needed health services that should, in a just world, be available to all women. Without that, the system must surely be deficient and the parallel requirements more fragile.

The fourth requirement is the most obvious and frequently cited, though it must stand in parallel with the others.

There is also a fifth requirement, not found in the Cairo outcomes, perhaps because it isn't medical. In many poor communities worldwide, children had great importance as those who would care for their parents in their old age. To have only one or two children in such communities lowered very much the likelihood of parents being sustained in their old age. Children were a form of insurance. To remove that need, some form of pension for the aged is required.

The United Nations Population Fund (UNFPA)

The UNFPA is key to making good the population policy just described. UNFPA's written objective is to "deliver a world where every pregnancy is wanted, every childbirth is safe and every young person's potential is fulfilled," and it advises countries that this route is the best route to attain sustainable development. UNFPA is also one of the world's largest funders of population data collection. In his book *Common Wealth* (2008) Jeffrey Sachs says of UNFPA that it needs greatly expanded funding; and that it is "the focal point for the effort to stabilize the global population at eight billion by 2015." That objective remains, except that it didn't happen by 2015.

Population data and projections

Readers are warned that almost all published projections of global population beyond the present are uncertain and become very unreliable beyond about 20 years ahead, perhaps because demographers do not take into account the changing carrying capacities of countries to sustain population. In many cases these capacities are themselves diminishing, invalidating models that tacitly assume constant capacities. In particular, projections of global population to the year 2050 and beyond are most unreliable, since there are great uncertainties in projections of food production by such times, and there is no evidence in published data that food production has been included in demographic modeling.

Population age distributions corresponding to long-lived populations

It is well known from demographic studies that populations with low birth rates and high expectation of life have age distributions lacking the very wide base of young people found in countries having high birth rates. This has sometimes given rise to the comment that societies having large percentages of people over 60 will have a shortage of people to serve as care givers for the aged. The evidence is rather that such countries tend also to have a maximum of unemployed among young adults, so that overall availability of workers is not in question. There can of course be a shortage of people who *wish* to enter employment in caring for the aged, but, in a fully ecological economy, health will be much improved compared with the present, and we may even find that being over 65 no longer qualifies as "aged."

Conclusion

It is essential that global population come to its maximum as soon as possible and then begin a decline. Any other course will guarantee the elimination of vast numbers of species, which are already in steep decline; and will render more difficult the already colossal challenge of addressing climate change.

Several countries globally are in population decline or at the verge of a decline. Japan's decline is appropriate in view of its high ecological footprint. Population declines are worthy of study because of imagined fears that declining population implies economic recession. Such a correlation may or may not occur in a neoliberal economy, but will not likely be found in an ecological economy where there is a focus on maintaining the good health of the ecosphere.

Notes

1. The quotation marks here indicate merely my skepticism on the merits of certain aspects of modern farming and of modern medicine.

2. www.footprintnetwork.org/resources

3. Jared Diamond *Collapse: How Societies Choose to Fail or Succeed* The Penguin Group 2005.

4. Lack of evidence for war prior to 4300 BC is noted in the author's chapter "Democratic Governance: the need for equal representation of women" on page 246 in E Diener and D R Rahtz *Advances in Quality of Life Theory and Research* Kluwer Academic Publishers 2000 pp. 243-60.

5. Roundtable on Food and Population, cohosted by the Global Issues Project (see Appendix 2) and Ryerson University.

6. The United Nations organized four world conferences on women. These took place in Mexico City in 1975, Copenhagen in 1980, Nairobi in 1985 and Beijing in 1995. The last was followed by a series of five-year reviews.

7. The International Conference on Population and Development (ICPD) 1994.

Chapter Seventeen

Farming, Food and Human Health

One of the benefits of an ecological economy is that it will be able to cope with the desperate state of farming on small farms in much of the world [1]. Farming is essential, but its continuance on a family scale is uncertain, though some farmers these past seventy years have had considerable financial success by sharing tasks and costly machinery among several medium-sized farms. The case against agribusiness, with its concentration of huge monocultures and excessive use of fertilizers and pesticides has been made again and again and will not be repeated here. Nevertheless, it is worth restating Joel Bourne's remark that, following the 2008 food crisis, "the green revolution was over, leaving unsustainable monocultures and ecological destruction in its wake." [2] The immense advantages of organic growing are by now well established, but the ability to produce more than agribusiness can produce per acre is still rare with organic farming, which thus cannot replace the current monoculture agribusiness in the medium-short term, which is unfortunate having regard to the aims of the ecological economy [3].

What the EE can provide are the requirements for improving soil for organic growing. And this has to be a priority. The matter of increasing wealth has been introduced in Chapter Six, and the preparations (measured in years) for organic growing provide yet another example. Organic growing is an important example because it will tend to optimize human health and the condition of the ecosphere.

Health

In Chapter Ten there is a brief discussion of food from an industrial point of view applying, *inter alia*, to food processing. Here we can look briefly at the relevance of organic farming, as its future may be within an ecological economy; will it make a difference? Though the changes will take time, I am convinced that we shall see an improvement in nutritive value of foods, including a restoration of full vitamin and mineral contents to levels experienced prior to agribusiness and its monocultures.

It is true that foods having all the benefits referred to here already can be found in health food stores in many developed countries, but these outlets developed precisely because products of the desired qualities were mainly unavailable from normal food shops and supermarkets.

Next will follow the food price debate. Will people who have become used to food being very cheap [4] be prepared to pay the extra? This cannot be answered now, but the overall growth of organic production continues, which is good news. Real costs are so very often hidden in the traditional economy, for example, threats to the ecosystem itself.

Agribusiness is plagued with most complex problems arising, for example, from neonicotinoids in pesticides [5]. A relatively recent example arising from agribusiness is the devastating effect on bees of the use of glyphosate in weed killers. Glyphosate is also known to have serious negative effects on human health [6]. The function of bees in the natural world is of huge importance, and cannot be measured in currency. Such are the many externalities that the traditional economy ignores.

One can also ask, "Why the inaction of ministers of health on important questions that, while not presenting immediate dangers, nevertheless affect long-term human health?" Chapter Twelve mentions MacLeans Magazine's May 6, 2014 issue on the dangers of excess sugar, which was entirely well documented and convincing. Three years later, can anyone see any difference in processed food marketing as a result? Could it be that the needed policy changes would interfere with profit? In an ecological economy, health would come first. And it is doubly important that this should be so, since the challenges faced by the human race are going to increase these next years.

Notes

1. Joel K Bourne *The End of Plenty: the race to feed a crowded world* W W Norton and Company 2015. On pp. 9-11 he gives glimpses of the difficulties of farming in the United States, enough to discourage almost anyone from continuing in his farmer-father's footsteps. The risks of ruin were simply too great. This book is the most important non-fiction out of the great mass of recent work I have been obliged to examine since preparing to write on ecological economics.

2. Joel K Bourne *loc. cit.* Chapter 12 "Organic Agriculture"

3. Joel K Bourne *loc. cit.*

4. For those who don't think supermarket food cheap nowadays (in prosperous, developed countries), they only need to refer back to food prices in, say, the 1950s, which they will find relatively expensive if they do their estimations in currencies corrected for the intervening inflation.

5. https://en.wikipedia.org/wiki/Neonicotinoid

6. See Stephanie Seneff's 2013 video on YouTube: https://www.youtube.com/watch?v=qYC6oyBglZI

Chapter Eighteen

Militarism

Among the world's many faulty social structures, militarism stands out as the most dangerous; it could condemn civilization to its end in an hour or so. And it has been sapping planetary resources for decades.

Militarism is a state of mind, born and bred through experience, and very permanent in the minds of those who have acquired it. It can put peace out of reach. Yet it is possible to overcome dominant military influence. More than once, peace has been attained and long preserved in parts of the world where formerly there had been animosity and warfare.

Anatol Rapoport, wrote a classic paper for a conference on the defense of Europe in 1985 [1]. An aim of the conference was to draw attention to disarmament of "conventional" weapons, since the peace movement at that time had been strongly focused on nuclear disarmament. Yet, as one of the military experts pointed out at that time, the millions of people killed in armed struggles during the 40 years since the Nagasaki bomb was dropped in 1945, had all been killed by "conventional" weapons, by which he excluded nuclear, chemical and biological weapons. It was also known by then that the vast majority of casualties and deaths in those wars were civilian.

Rapoport's paper is of great generality. In it he says, "None of the time-honored extra-military war aims are worth a war fought with modern weapons of total destruction: not conquest of territory, not trade monopolies, not the imposition of an ideology, not the enslavement of a population. The material costs of modern war must exceed by several orders of magnitude any material benefits." A few pages further on: "Defence? Whom do military establishments defend? There were, to be sure, eras when armies defended their countries from marauders and rapacious invaders . . . But throughout most of this modern era this has seldom been so. Armies, when on the defensive have primarily defended themselves, not populations. And populations have been victimized by their own armies as well as the enemy's."

In 1945, the United Nations was created, and this was the most significant global development in international relations since the earliest civilizations. For the first time, national governments everywhere were being invited to treat others as they would like to be treated—on an International scale.

What has changed since then and what in particular has gone wrong? The list is long, so here's only a partial one. First, the belief in a few countries that they can prevail militarily, and thus fulfill political ambitions to dominate others (none of whom wants to be dominated). Second, the sponsorship of cruel surrogate wars during the long US-USSR confrontation—the Cold War [2]. Third, the failure to disarm multilaterally, which was the purpose of the three Special Sessions of the United Nations (1978, 83 and 88). Fourth, a host of unjustifiable and destructive military interventions. Fifth, the continued development of more and more new types of weapon, including such as permit internationally illegal, violent action from a distance. Sixth, the failure to distinguish between force (which is sometimes necessary) and violence, which is always to be avoided [3].

Nobody has immediate, practical answers to these dilemmas, as otherwise the problems might well have been resolved by now.

There are also other, newer types of issue in the realm of conflict, of which cyber warfare needs mention. Cyber war has been defined by author Richard Clarke as "actions by a nation state to penetrate another nation's computers or networks for the purposes of causing damage or disruption." [4] One can extend the definition to attack by non-state actors, but then one might prefer to call it cyber crime. Either can be very dangerous, considering the state of armament of some nations, especially those having nuclear weapons. The problem (as always) is: what to do about it? Cyber crime has been with us for many years, though we called it hacking most of the time, and it is still unsolved—we do not see the criminal and haven't learned how to catch him. My view is that the threat of cyber war is yet another message to humanity to cease international rivalry, thereby eliminating cyber war and enabling us to collaborate against cyber crime. The collaboration will be most important, because the effects of cyber crime could be as bad as those of cyber war. A regime of prevention must surely be possible, and would also protect businesses and private computer systems.

The world of rapid communications now depends almost exclusively on systems established in outer space on near-Earth satellites. Such a system will always be vulnerable, since satellites can be targeted and destroyed, or can suffer an accident in outer space. Though there are at least two countries having technology capable of destroying the orbiting satellites of another state, it is not in the interests of any nation having such technology to use it that way. The threat could, however, arise if a nation so equipped were threatened so seriously with its own destruction that it would act out of desperation. The very complex space system therefore remains vulnerable enough that a parallel communications system—one not dependent on outer space—is really necessary in case of emergency. These matters are, however, independent of whether an ecological economy is in place, but the ecological economy requires a regime of peace, as does the human race if it wants to come out of its present predicaments alive and well; and peace is a huge step forward toward reducing the threats just discussed.

It has been noted, for example by Project Ploughshares, Canada's only major peace research institute, that wars between nations are on the decline, so that the remaining armed conflicts are internal national conflicts, and, as time progresses, more and more complex in their composition of rival groups. The increasing complexity is not easy to deal with, but surely a more collaborative international climate will ease such problems. The armed struggles are very troublesome, especially as they are increasingly displacing people, in addition to all the other depredations of conflict. I therefore conclude this section with a few points and questions on some of the world's unresolved conflicts. The attack on Afghanistan when the Taliban were in control failed in the sense that the Taliban are still fighting. The overly violent British-American invasion of Iraq did huge harm and has not brought about a general stability there, since it gave birth to ISIS, which in turn made a resolution of the Syrian crisis much more painful. Does the current war perpetrated by Saudi Arabia against Yemen have any justification? Do the Kurds have to be military targets of aggression in any and all countries in which they live? These last examples illustrate stronger nations attacking weaker neighbors or ethnic groups within their boundaries in overpopulated areas of the world.

If there is a solution to such aggression, it requires the recognition by relevant leaders and their cabinets that their policies are not working. The Nationalist Party of South Africa stopped its apartheid policy when one of its leaders recognized that apartheid was not working. Thirty years earlier, you could never have convinced any member of the Nationalist Party their apartheid policy could fail.

The above list barely touches upon the ways in which militaristic policies fail; and in which policies to control others fail.

More evidence that national military policies are failing comes from the failure to address climate change, the fast-increasing numbers of refugees, the decline of species, and the dying ocean, and the failure to create sustainable societies [5]. This is because all major issues are interrelated; and **every resource put into military violence in this over-armed world adds emphasis to the failures**.

The new phrase, the redeeming principle is *international cooperation*.

Notes

1. Anatol Rapoport "Whose Security does Defence defend?" in *Defending Europe: Options for Security* Taylor and Francis 1986 pp. 271-80.

2. The Cold War between the USA and its allies and the Soviet Union lasted for four decades starting very soon after the defeat of Germany in 1945. It got its name from the fact that there was no military aggression between the two sides during all those years, but the many threatening confrontations continued past the 1970s and were heightened to a crisis by the election of Ronald Reagan as President of the United States (November 1979), the failure of the USA to sign the long-awaited treaty on nuclear arms limitation (SALT 2), the Soviet invasion of Afghanistan (late December 1979), and the US decision the same year to target Soviet Missile silos instead of cities

with their intercontinental missiles, which was interpreted in the USSR as a move to make possible a US nuclear first strike. Although there was no direct, violent aggression US-USSR, both sides armed and supported different parties in other violent conflicts, such as the first part of the civil war in Angola (1975-91).

3. The distinction is emphasized in Ely Culbertson's *Total Peace* Doubleday Doran and Company 1943.

4. Richard A Clarke *Cyber War* Harper Collins

5. Wackernagel's Footprint News annually reports the world's regression away from sustainability. See Appendix 3 Ecological Footprint.

Chapter Nineteen

Inequalities: Income and Power

Inequality has most often been presented in terms of the incomes of the best-off and worst-off individuals in a given society. Economists sometimes assess inequality by computing the average income in each income decile of a given population; a simple measure of inequality then becomes the ratio of averages of the top and bottom deciles.

This type of inequality grew slightly in the 1970s, and then more rapidly since then, especially in the United States and Canada, and shows no signs of leveling off. If one projects the current trend far enough, it leads eventually to the appalling prospect of unnecessary human poverty for the great majority of people.

Much has been written on inequality of incomes by Thomas Piketty [1], coauthors Richard Wilkinson and Kate Pickett [2], and Joseph Stiglitz [3]. Stiglitz explains the social inequalities in terms of politics: the failure of democracy. If the rich can influence policy so that they receive an increasing share of the pie, this produces more and more inequality. Inequality is surely unjust, but is it eroding the law? Clearly Stiglitz thinks it is in the USA.

Piketty uses the statistics of income, salary, benefits, salary deductions and all taxes to show that the inequalities are roughly proportional to salary inequalities in Europe, the USA and Canada. He makes no specific recommendations, but thinks the inequalities must be reduced. He defines what he calls *taux effectifs marginaux* (effective marginal rates), which can be applied to salaries, additional benefits, salary deductions and taxes, so as to compute how much someone gains in net finances by climbing out of a lower salary group to a higher. He claims that the lowest salary decile gains the least because of stiff deductions and/or loss of benefits, and says that governments would do well to make this situation less discouraging.

Wilkinson and Pickett provide many data showing some correlation (but nowhere strong correlation) between the rich-poor income gap and other undesirable social measures, but their strength is in their various conclusions. They and Piketty agree that the central problem is salary spread between the richest and poorest of the employed, which is too great.

The three books span 800 pages, with over 1000 references and a bibliography of over 120 books, all of which has led nowhere so far. Let's therefore have a fresh look at the problem, its historical context, how the present inequality was so easily achieved, and what could now be done about it.

A huge historical error of western civilization was to largely deregulate banks [4] while allowing continuance of profit-making as the sole objective of corporations, including banks, and of other conditions described below. For many years, major corporations had already shown great skill at bargaining for good conditions, including subsidies and low taxes, when they wanted to set up manufacturing. Most countries wanted manufacturing set up within their territory, because of the employment and increased taxes (however modest), so they agreed to the conditions. The process is competitive in that other countries also want the manufacturing within their jurisdiction, and the "contract" goes to the lowest bidder—the one who offers the most and wants the least in tax. It became a race to the bottom, with wealthy corporations paying as little as seven percent tax on huge profits. Tax avoidance is further exacerbated by tax havens. The subject of tax havens is complex, but the type of tax haven referred to here is made possible by a country that has set up a legal process through which a corporation can claim to have established plant and/or head offices there, while those physical entities may not be found there at all. Such conditions accentuate the continuing widening distribution of individual wealth.

This whole picture was preventable, and can be reversed.

Containing this kind of corporate behavior requires the heads of states to agree on terms that they require of businesses, including the dismantling of tax havens, or agreement not to use them. Also there will likely have to be severe penalties for infringement of such agreements. The current situation arose because governments saw each other as in competition, and were thus exploitable, whereas they need to be cooperating on the road to prosperity—world prosperity, not just local prosperity, something that is essential in the ecological economy.

At the same time, corporate profit is a general good and is needed globally if pensions are to be provided where they are needed, a continually changing picture as expectation of life increases globally, which it has been doing for a long time. A new look at taxing corporations is called for, one that incorporates thresholds as in personal income taxation, and justly takes into account corporate size.

Returning now briefly to inequality, what might be an acceptable goal? Most employees in most occupations earn less than one *Sal*, where the Sal is a top annual salary for someone in government or public life or any of the bureaucracies; one might think of it for convenience as the President's (or the Prime Minister's) annual salary. Maybe the world could live with a system in which the Sal was twelve times the minimum yearly wage based upon a 36-hour week, and nobody had more annual spending income than a few Sal [5].

The inequality problem stems from the fact that the corporate wealthy have managed to create a new class of super-rich, analogous to but not at all resembling the aristocracy of the nineteenth century. The Sal becomes a pittance in this class. The new aristocracy uses its power to increase its monetary wealth both intelligently and mindlessly. Intelligently, because it knows very well how to increase that monetary wealth, and because some corporations are doing most admirable things in this world. Mindlessly, because other corporations have no regard for health as broadly discussed in this book, and some are contributing hugely to what could very soon become an irreversible climate disaster.

To restore the needed balance of power between governments, collectively, and corporations, the former will have to collaborate to agree on a new *Carta Magna* of terms for the new rich, the reverse of the process in 1215, when it was the ruler who had to be held in check by the aristocracy [6]. In so doing, governments will need to be prepared (and if necessary legislate) to remove corporate charters in cases of serious environmental damage. A plan to address climate change can be made more specific at the same time.

The rest is detail. Some of it will be in the *Carta Magna*, more to follow later.

Notes

1. Thomas Piketty *L'économie des inégalités* Editions la Découverte.2015. This book exists in an English translation, *The Economics of Inequality* (2015).

2. Richard Wilkinson and Kate Pickett *The Spirit Level: Why Equality is Better for Everyone* Penguin 2010.

3. Joseph E Stiglitz *The Price of Inequality: how today's divided society endangers our future* W W Norton and Company 2012.

4. https://en.wikipedia.org/wiki/Big_Bang_(financial_markets)

5. Very large incomes or earnings will not be avoidable, unless the mean-spirited want to deny successful and remarkable people, whose incomes are surely in excess of a few Sal, the pleasure of using their wealth constructively. Issues of this kind can be handled through investment directives, which, in the ecological economy, might include some special requirements.

6. This concept is essential to the ecological economy, to bring us to a sustainable existence and to do it fast enough to avoid the climate transition, and the continuing increase in inequality.

Chapter Twenty

Using New Indices of Wealth and Prosperity

There are two traditional issues here. One is the familiar list of objections to GDP (gross domestic product) as an indicator to prosperity, and the other is the need for an index of human welfare.

In the ecological economy we shall need indices of resource wealth and of the state of living things on this planet. Indicators of human welfare will also be most useful.

Fiscal indices

The fiscal index used about everywhere at present is the gross domestic product. It is defined as the monetary value of all finished goods produced and services supplied within a country's borders in a given time, usually one year. It thus measures the money exchanged within a country, except within families or between friends or within the underground economy, that is, the trading that goes on without official records. Investopedia gives the following formula for calculating GDP:

GDP = C + G + I + NX

Where C is private consumer spending, G is the sum of spending by governments, I is the sum of the country's investment, including businesses' capital expenditures, and NX is the total of exports minus imports, in fiscal terms.

This index is considered important as a measure of relative prosperity, but has been hugely criticized in that it is calculated without regard to how or why the expenditures were made. There are dozens of examples of such objections [1], but I will only mention two. When disaster hits a country, and huge sums must be spent to restore capital assets, and there may also be great losses of natural wealth, GDP usually rises, because it measures the costs of the repairs and reconstruction, and it ignores any loss of natural and built wealth. Again, though its aim is to indicate prosperity, it has nothing to say about the state of contentment of the people. Consumerism will increase GDP, but may not give any increase in human happiness, and it can cause considerable pollution of the environment.

A claimed improvement on GDP is the net domestic product, which subtracts depreciation of assets from the GDP formula, and therefore represents more accurately the fiscal aspect of prosperity. But net domestic product has not caught on, in the sense that all governments and economists continue to quote GDP, which hides so many important details. The net domestic product would also hide all of those details except depreciation and built-capital losses due to disasters.

Wealth measurement in an ecological economy

Here we are on uncertain ground, as nobody knows what will emerge in an ecological economy, except that it will not be money-centered, mentally speaking. And it is the concentration on purely fiscal matters that shows so very strongly and clearly the failure of the traditional economy.

The requirements in an ecological economy will be to measure and keep track of capital resources, including natural resources. This is already done for forest lumber in some jurisdictions. And it is most important, since the living planet depends on forest as well as the ocean for its oxygen. But forest resources are also closely tied to human development; and forest provides much habitat for other species.

Fish stocks will be important, and species of all sorts, since they are mostly threatened today or in steep decline. Environmental information is often found in the hands of nongovernmental organizations, and it remains to be seen what kind of relationships will develop between such organizations and the emancipated future governments that will be emerging from their traditional roles into the new era of full life.

An idea of natural wealth accounting at government level can be obtained from the work of NRTEE [2].

Index of human wellbeing

In Daly and Cobb's book *For the Common Good* (1989) there is an Appendix on an index of economic welfare. Max-Neef mentions [3], however, that their index has morphed into the Genuine Progress Index

(GPI). The GPI, also now widely called the Genuine Progress Indicator, is discussed in Nickerson's book, already cited [4], and elsewhere. Guardian Sustainable Business [5] states that 20 US states have already adopted the Genuine Progress Indicator as a substitute for GDP. In 2012, Vermont was the first state to pass into law this new metric for measuring economic prosperity. The difference between GDP and GPI is that GPI subtracts many negative factors from the GDP that amount, like ghg emissions, to damage to the ecological system, or to the health of our social system. One of the subtracted factors in determining the GPI comes from inequality. Altogether, there are 26 elements combined in the GPI.

GPI needs to increase as long as there is abject poverty or dire poverty, but a point must come rather soon in the global future when the totals of GDP and GPI for all countries cease to rise and begin to decline in sync with a decline of human population.

The growth factor

It might appear at first sight that GPI is "the" solution to measurement of prosperity within an ecological economy. It is certainly looking good, as it represents a huge advance on GDP, but we must be cautious, because the growth element, that is the belief that "growth is good *per se*" persists in the jurisdictions using the GPI. Thus. until now, GPI remains a creature of the traditional system, albeit a system trying to reform itself. Tim Jackson [6] and Peter Victor [7] have separately and jointly been doing splendid pioneer work to convince people in business that economic growth is not a necessary feature of a healthy economy. Herman Daly has also joined this throng [8]. This theme is a prologue to setting up an ecological economy.

Notes

1. Mike Nickerson's *Life Money and Illusion* 2006 has over 20 references to GDP, almost all highly negative.

2. National Roundtable on the Environment and the Economy (NRTEE) *Environment and Sustainable Development indicators for Canada* Renouf Publishing Ltd 2003 ISBN 1-894737-06-7.

3. Philip B Smith and Manfred Max-Neef *Economics unmasked* Green Books 2011 Chapter 10 (threshold hypothesis).

4. Mike Nickerson *loc. cit.* pp. 223-25. Nickerson and colleagues have been pursuing the notion of of a genuine progress index (GPI) these many years, which reached the stage of a parliamentary motion in Ottawa, which passed with a large majority in 2003, but was not acted upon by government.

5. https://www.theguardian.com/sustainable-business/2014/sep/23

6. Tim Jackson *Prosperity Without Growth: Economics for a Finite Planet* Earthscan 2009.

7. Peter Victor *Managing Without Growth: Slower by Design, Not Disaster* Edward Elgar Publishing 2008.

8. Herman E Daly *From Uneconomic Growth to a Steady-State Economy* Edward Elgar Publishing 2014.

Chapter Twenty-One

China

China and India account for more than one third of the world's human population and both are fast developing economically. While India's development is at a comparatively early stage, China's has leapt forward, reducing poverty by a factor greater than 40 in under 40 years, and has developed and is still developing a great many industries and much export business. This chapter discusses China, since it poses two vital questions.

China's booming economy

China began its astonishing build-up of civil industry in 1978, following policy changes at the end of its rule by the so-called Gang of Four. Between then and now, the economy has grown at an astonishing pace, recently becoming the world's largest industrial economy, as measured by GDP, the indicator that China chose to use. From 2007-2015 it achieved an astonishing growth rate of over 15 percent annually, though dropping to about 5.5 percent in 2015 [1], and now continuing at about the same rate.

Poverty elimination

The growth rapidly brought the population out of poverty—the lot of over half a billion rural Chinese in 1978—leaving fewer than 25 million in poverty in 2017. This great achievement is reflected in the Human Development Index (HDI) for China, which rose steadily from about 0.42 in 1980 to 0.718 in 2010, about the world average, and then more slowly until it reached 0.738 in 2016.

Fueling China's electrical needs

The remarkable economic growth was fuelled by coal, a resource China has in plenty within its territory. Most of China's electrical power came from coal-fired power stations, which were built at a great pace. Today (2017), with some coal-fired power stations operating at only 44 percent of full capacity, and people protesting against the excessive air pollution in their cities, permission for constructing new coal-fired plant is rarely given.

Reliable data allow one to make projections of electrical supplies to the year 2020, which ends the current five-year plan. The numbers are shown in the 2020 column of table 21.1. The electrical output from coal is colossal at 1100 GWe (gigawatt electrical) and the other numbers are all large compared with what one would find in other jurisdictions. For wind and photovoltaic (PV) energy conversion, my sources gave only the installed capacities, so I had to estimate the likely electrical outputs. Though the PV output is the lowest, the progress in solar PV in China is impressive. The solar intensity at the Earth's surface is barely 1 kW/m^2, and the efficiency of conversion of solar to electric power is at best 30 percent, so we need at least 3.3 square meters of panels to produce 1 kW at noon on a sunny day. But the average sunshine intensity is only one third of this; therefore the 39 GWe average in table 21.1 requires a noon maximum of 130 GWe. The installation to do this require at least 130 X 3.3 = 430 square km of panels!

Greenhouse gas emissions

In 2015, China's emissions amounted to 10.6 GT (gigatonnes) of carbon dioxide, or 27 percent of the world's huge total, while its population numbered under 18 percent of the global total. Where is this headed? By 2015, the rate of growth of China's emissions had slowed but the emissions themselves are not likely to peak until 2029 [2], at which time the output could be close to 13 Gt per annum, implying a continuing huge CO_2 output until well after that date. These factors induced me to construct table 21.1, and they call for added emphasis here to recommendations in Chapter Twenty-Two under the subheading Climate change.

Further projections of China's energy mix

This section presents table 21.1, which is only intended to illustrate a possible future in electrical supply. Projections become less reliable beyond 2020, because of uncertainty in the continued growth of some of the energy sources. For similar reasons, projections beyond 2030 contain much guesswork. It is expected that the population will peak in 2031 [3]. One can speculate that electrical production will also peak at or before that time, but that its subsequent decline will be slow. The numbers for nuclear power are based upon installed capacities multiplied by optimistic fractional average outputs for such installations; while the installed capacities are based upon building plans to 2030.

Table 21.1

Electrical projections to 2050, in GWe

Year	2020	2030	2050
Coal-fired	1,100	900 ?	300 ?
Gas-fired	110	220 ?	220 ?
Hydroelectric	340	340	340
Wind	50	80 ?	204 ?
Solar PV	39	84	84 ?
Solar concentration	0	?	80 ?
Nuclear	47	79	240
Total	1,686 ?	1,704 ?	1,468 ?
Renewable subtotal	439	505 ?	718 ?

The question marks indicate the less certain estimates or guesswork, the other numbers being justifiable from present knowledge. The 204 GWe for wind power in 2050 is less than half China's exploitable wind capacity (2,380 GW) converted at 22 percent to give electrical output. The solar PV power could grow between 2030 and 2050. Should China develop its maximum wind capacity, wind could in principle eliminate coal from the mix, assuming a total power generation below 1500 GWe. These results are of course very rough, but we are talking of a 33-year forward look, which is inevitably subject to major uncertainty.

Is China's economy fully ecological?

The type of economy China has chosen doesn't fit any standard picture. It follows the path of a very successful neoliberal economy, with important differences. It has brought the great mass of the population out of poverty, and has successfully tackled major projects in renewable energy while arguing the need to preserve its environment. It also would appear to have embraced the concept of preserving a healthy environment globally. It built these successes, however, on an enormous base of coal power, and the country is now paying the price through its medical costs arising from the pollution of city air, and its huge challenge to eliminate ghg emissions from fossil fuels. It is also taking the risks that accompany adoption of nuclear power, a Faustian bargain. All in all, China is perhaps more than halfway to becoming an ecological economy, but we must look at the growth question.

China's GDP growth, at least to 2010, was necessary to bring people out of poverty, and there is still some need for more growth, since there is still a remnant of that former poverty; but for how long will it require a growth rate of about six percent annually? Although this seems small compared with the 15 percent of the years 2000-2014, six percent compounded means a doubling of the economy in only 17 years. Is that necessary, or even desirable? Given that the population is likely to peak around 2031, the need for GDP growth could by then be negligible.

The Chinese emphasis on growth, however, mimics the traditional belief that growth is good *per se*, and may thus be an example of what Herman Daly calls *growthmania* [4], or what Richard Douthwaite calls *growth imperative* [5]. Douthwaite studied England's economy from the 18th century up to 1910, and noticed that the spurts of intensive growth, when industry was already well developed, enriched the capitalists, but didn't benefit the labor they employed. By contrast, the work force tended to benefit more from the periods of slow growth. Clearly China's present growth rate benefits many entrepreneurs but, might the work force do better in a slower-growth mode? This is not to say that China's economy is an historical cycle following England's past mode, but merely that it could be useful to see whether the lot of workers in China is in any way related to the growth rate. The ecological economist will accept the eventual degrowth of an economy, as the population subsides. Degrowth, however, is likely not in anyone's mind in today's China.

Another special feature of China's economy is the official attitude to employment. In China there is an annual entry into the job market of about 15 million young people who have finished their schooling or other studies. The regime wants to see them usefully employed. This provides a need to expand the economy further. What indicates the nature of the economy is the selection of employment. If all enter into profit-oriented enterprises, then the approach is traditional (or neoliberal); if a substantial number work to improve natural wealth and other conditions of humanity and of the ecosphere, then it indicates the ecological option.

China's economy must already be close to the point where most of the increase in production must be exported. China is a very successful exporter, partly because it controls its exchange rate to make sales favorable and maintains (seen from the rest of the world) a low minimum wage. However, the very success of those exports can increase unemployment elsewhere. In the 1980s, the late Eric Kierans, a former Minister of Finance in Canada, said how all nations would love to export their unemployment [6]. He was referring exactly to this phenomenon we can see in China's future, though it may be that no one in China has yet seen it in that light. Because modern production methods can produce all the goods that people need with a small fraction of the world's total workforce, maintaining one's own people employed *industrially* and exporting very extensively in fact implies creating unemployment elsewhere. This is one of the reasons for general adoption of an ecological economy, since the job market will then include employment in ecological projects.

Chinese commercial success has been additionally assisted by hoarding US currency and gold, as well as lending huge amounts to the US Government. This success was aided and abetted by entrepreneurs from western civilization who fell for the short-term benefit to themselves of producing abroad where labor was cheap. China has succeeded better at keeping production at home than the English during the heyday of their colonial empire. Some Chinese documents reveal their writers' thinking on keeping production local [2,7].

Postscript

Questions remain. Will China succeed in greening its energy supplies through existing technology sufficiently to make the path to zero emissions evident by 2050? Since this is uncertain, China might do well to revive its geothermal energy program [8]. It is already making progress with an important project for energy conversion by solar concentration, which gives the opportunity of storing heat (for example, in small rocks) at high temperature so as to produce electric power continuously, throughout the hours without sunshine. Though China has entered this field, it has adopted the tower method, which uses multiple, movable mirrors, a technology that is far more expensive than solar panels—per kWhr generated. Professional inventor J Varga's untried method of solar concentration using rotatable Fresnel lenses has been thoroughly costed to be very much cheaper than the tower method, competitive with the cheapest methods of electrical generation [9]. Solar concentration is best suited to hot climates where the average solar heat flux is greatest, within and near the tropics; it has the potential to provide electric power for over half the world's population.

Notes

1. World Bank data.

2. Xinhua News Agency *Green China Green Economy* 2016. The estimate of 5.4 percent annual increases in greenhouse gas emissions is elsewhere stated to be 3.3 percent, and these numbers are hard to verify, because they depend on small differences between large numbers having appreciable uncertainties. It is also important to recognize from Chinese data, that when they say "emissions are down by such and such percent by comparison with 2005," this is not at all what is meant! It means that the increase in emissions was less than the increase in GDP by that percentage!

3. http://www.worldometers.info/world-population/china-population/

4. Herman E Daly *From Uneconomic Growth to a Steady-State Economy* Edward Elgar 2014.

5. Richard Douthwaite *The Growth Illusion* Council Oak Books 1993.

6. The Hon. Eric Kierans, 1987, private communication on the question of unemployment in a work in progress of his at that time.

7. Nuclear Power in China: http://www.world-nuclear.org/information-library/country-profiles/countries-a-f/china-nuclear-power.aspx

8. Wikipedia's 4 June 2017 article on geothermal power in China mentions a program to obtain over 7,700 MW of power from geothermal sources. The program has, however, not been started.

9. J M J Varga, former president of Crosrol Ltd, UK, private communication c.2011-May 2017

Chapter Twenty-Two

Recommendations

In this chapter, the notes are numbered according to the recommendations. The first group comprises general recommendations that are at the heart of ecological economics.

Throughout the remaining recommendations, there are many in the form of calls for further study. In most cases, it did not seem appropriate to name categories of individuals, groups or government departments who might need to undertake such studies. These recommendations are therefore in the nature of invitations to study and examine the stated matters.

Recommendations

Those numbered 1, 2 and 3 head the list because their fulfillment will assist in a general way to set up an ecological economy. The failure of traditional economics to identify clearly the *necessity* for essentially full employment and the *need* to "restore the commons" etc. are prime reasons why this book had to be written.

General recommendations

1. That the United Nations Economic and Social Council prepare a Declaration to be signed by all UN member nations that world economic affairs both within and among nations shall henceforth be conducted on the basis that the health and wellbeing of the ecosphere and of humanity shall be the overriding priority for the future of this planet, and that every human being shall be taught this *general principle* as an educational right.

2. That every nation and/or federation of nations shall create a national (or regional) publicly owned bank (or system of such banks) or equivalent organization to enable the *general principle* to be realized.

Note 2. The use of the word *bank* here means institution that has the right and duty to issue new money for essential purposes, such as restoring the commons, and other wealth-enhancement projects as may at different times appear necessary to the governors of the said institution. Implicitly, the governors must be highly qualified and intelligent in their choice of projects, and must listen to and seek the advice of nongovernmental groups as well as others having knowledge in the appropriate fields.

2a. That in the absence of such publicly owned bank, as proposed in recommendation 2, the national treasury shall be used to create necessary funds for the realization and fulfillment of the *general principle*.

2b. That nations break from the imposed BIS rules against using national banks for issuing loans at "nominal" interest or interest-free.

Note 2b. The BIS rules were undoubtedly brought into existence for what seemed at the time sound reasons, but they have contributed to ever-increasing indebtedness of governments in recent times. The state of the planet demands a change from this, and financing of the change must be at zero or near-zero interest, not only because of the long history of neglect of the commons and increasing pollution of the globe, but also because the recent phase of the traditional system has put governments and individuals so deeply into debt.

2c. That, in the case of nations that are poor in natural resources, arrangements be pursued to provide funds generated as per recommendation 2 by the most prosperous countries.

Note 2c. The purpose of this recommendation is to enable poor countries to purchase resources needed for the fulfillment of the *general principle*. In an ecological economy, resources are to be the limiting factors, not money.

2d. That indebted governments everywhere make immediate efforts to reduce, or negotiate with a view to reducing debt, especially foreign debt.

Note 2d. This recommendation is intended to render 2c more realizable.

Full employment

3. That all nations forthwith develop full employment policies by establishing wealth creating projects along lines parallel to the kind of suggestions proffered in Chapter Six; and implement the full employment policy without avoidable delay.

3a. That in fulfilling the objectives of recommendation 3, project managers/committees/etc. pay close attention to the need of full employment for youth, especially in the age group 18-30; and that this process apply also to those who are in post-secondary education or training so that they can enjoy the benefits of employment during the years of their studies, outside college terms.

Planning

4. That all governments, especially national governments and state or provincial governments in geographically large jurisdictions, that do not have high-level roundtables with the mandate to look ahead 30 years create such roundtable(s) without delay.

Note 4. This recommendation arose from the conspicuous absence of such a roundtable among the very numerous roundtables of the Ontario Government, notwithstanding many difficulties facing that government, for example, in energy planning.

4a. That such roundtables be provided with highly sophisticated modeling services.

Note 4a. This recommendation arises from evidence of inadequate approaches to modeling, in matters such as projecting global population.

4b. That in addition to pursuing studies asked for by their respective government, such roundtables be free to investigate such problems as they deem necessary and advisable.

Note 4b. This recommendation arises from the excellence of reports from NRTEE, the National Roundtable on the Environment and the Economy in Ottawa.

4c. That planning for cities by city governments follow the precepts of 4 through 4b where practicable.

Note 4c. This recommendation arises from effects that are imposed upon cities from outside. An example is immigration, especially in countries that are accepting large numbers of refugees from war-torn regions of the world. Such influxes of people can be more than a city can deal with. The building trades do very nicely, but the city cannot widen the roads or revolutionize the city transportation to cope with the rapidly increasing population density. Long-term regional planning is needed, including the design of new cities and new types of inter-city transport. Much of this is missing in many jurisdictions at present, notwithstanding the presence of people capable of following through with such work.

Taxation

5. That taxes on services and on value-added should be abolished.

Note 5. Such taxes tend to augur against employment and thus against full employment, and therefore hinder the ecological economy.

5a. That studies be carried out nationally, and also internationally on the kind of measures suggested in Chapter Nineteen on reducing the span of incomes, while paying full attention to the needs for rational and fair corporate taxation, for which a just international code is needed.

5b. That nations form and pursue a joint policy of plugging tax loopholes.

Note 5b. This follows a general principle that taxes should be paid predominantly by those who can easily afford to so so.

5c. That tax-exempt business expenses everywhere be reviewed with a view to stricter limits, where they amount to loopholes.

Note 5c. This is necessary because people working for businesses are strongly favored in many jurisdictions within the traditional economic system compared with those not so employed—a systemic injustice.

5d. That business/corporate profits be subject to *as many tax thresholds* as are present personal income tax and surtax (or supertax) systems, and that corporate taxation be rationalized on a per employee basis.

Note 5d. This recommendation follows the logic (though not the reasons) of corporations wanting to be considered "persons" under the law. It follows that tax thresholds should be comparable with those on individuals, when profit is evaluated on a per-employee basis. Tax rates would also rise with per-employee profit. In this way a more just system of corporate taxation will be established. Here, "per employee" means per employee enjoying full benefits.

5e. That corporate law everywhere be changed to prevent "hostile" takeovers of businesses.

Note 5e. This recommendation follows from evidence that such takeovers benefit only very few individuals and can and often do have negative effects on the business taken over.

5f. That royalties be levied on materials extracted from the Earth's crust and from felling of trees, so as to favor the ecological principles: "reduce, re-use and recycle."

Note 5f. A specific example of such royalties arises from trees cut for wood pulp, to raise the price of new paper to that of recycled paper. In this way, the ecological economy would arrive at an optimum fraction of recycled material, and minimum wastage.

5g. That following the adoption of 5f, all sales tax would be lifted from such materials.

5h. That a major study be undertaken in all jurisdictions having stock markets within their bounds, the purpose being to evaluate the factors necessary to keep the fraction of money in circulation in the tertiary economy to a very modest and more-or-less constant fraction of the total, and to put into effect the necessary tax or other rules to bring about the desired result.

Note 5h. The tertiary economy is touched upon in Chapter Two and again in Chapter Four.

Climate change

6. That governments, industries, institutions and individuals move forward on climate change initiatives without waiting for the full establishment of an ecological economy, and without waiting for others to follow their lead in addressing climate change.

Note 6. This recommendation is particularly relevant in jurisdictions where government has chosen to ignore the threat of climate change!

6a. That everyone encourage and take part in much needed *conversations* among government, industries, institutions, nongovernmental organizations and individuals on how to accelerate the reductions of fossil-fuel burning, sector by economic sector, so as to bring these emissions to zero.

Note 6a. This recommendation follows from the normally longer-term planning of industries than the intervals between elections of politicians. Industries need to know what will be legally expected of them so as to plan what they can supply that will satisfy customers and remain in keeping with emissions-free technology.

6b. That all shall persuade governments to bring rapidly to zero, through direct policy, the fossil-fuel burning in those sectors of the economy where the technology to do so already exists.

Note 6b. This recommendation follows from Robert Hoffman's conclusions that it is too late to wait for a carbon tax to bring about the necessary reductions of emissions.

6c. That governments shall accelerate the cessation of fossil-fuel burning by ceasing to subsidize corporations in the fossil-fuel sectors and instead urge transition to other fields, where necessary offering subsidy to make the change.

Note 6c. This recommendation is widely supported by citizens but important governments continue to turn a deaf ear.

6d. That in several jurisdictions where there is currently manufacture of aircraft engines and engines for the propulsion of ocean-going ships, research and development should be undertaken on the development of non-polluting propulsion—involving zero emissions of greenhouse gases, with a view to using the newly developed engines in air and ocean transport within 15 years, and totally eliminating ghg-emitting air and ocean travel within 35 years.

Note 6d. This recommendation connects with Chapter Eleven, and addresses the dilemma of continuing some important elements of trade globalization and addressing the human strongly-felt need for travel. Chapter Eleven mentions oxygen-hydrogen, which is the only light-element, non-carbon fuel combination that makes any sense as a substitute for present-day fuels, and which happens to offer huge thermodynamic advantages. The alternatives to this recommendation are progressively heavier taxation of present aircraft and ship fuels or artificial restrictions on ocean and air transport, either of which would be found unacceptable by the huge numbers of people who would be affected. This recommendation is emphatically not intended to negate alternative routes to the elimination of ghg emissions, but **offers a choice that will work**, if the needed effort is put into the development.

6e. That an added focus on the reabsorption of carbon from the atmosphere is essential and must be brought into the public discussion by whatever means are available, and to the attention of governments.

Note 6e. This recommendation is largely neglected by the public and governments together, so far. It is most urgent.

6f. That governments study the claim of the Rodale Institute of having a method to sequester all the atmospheric CO_2 that needs to be removed from the atmosphere, and then pursue Rodale's plan wherever it can contribute to the desired effect.

Note 6f. The Rodale Institute announced 22 April 2014 the launch of a global campaign to generate public awareness of soil's ability to reverse climate change, but only when the health of the soil is maintained through organic regenerative agriculture. The campaign thus calls for the restructuring of our global food system with the goal of reversing climate change through photosynthesis and biology. This call falls within several aims of this book.

6g. That major studies be launched with a view to developing emissions-free production of cement for the concrete industry, with a view to replacing present plant at an early date.

Wealth creation

7. That nations, states, provinces, create bodies to study possibilities, within their own jurisdiction, for increasing natural wealth, and prepare to carry out such wealth-increasing programs, including making estimates of required equipment, resources and people to do the work in each program.

Note 7. A prime objective of an ecological economy.

7a. That the US Government demand of USDA, or another organization, a sound plan of action by which the waterways of Mississippi-Missouri basin could be cleaned up within a decade, with a view to eliminating the Gulf dead zone; and that it then supply the necessary resources to carry out that plan.

Note 7a. See Chapter Six. This is also a test case for financing at zero interest.

7b. That governments worldwide support major efforts toward afforestation wherever it makes scientific sense to do so.

Note 7b. See Chapter Six. Such support has long been given through international channels but needs to be greatly intensified, for example, by supplying appropriate resources.

7c. That the governments of Canada and Russia support further studies in the field to investigate the possibilities of afforestation north of the old tree line, and to fund trial plantations in those areas where adequate fire control can be maintained or introduced.

Note 7c. See Chapter Six.

7d. That governments worldwide generously support current efforts to stem the advance of the Sahara Desert in Africa.

Note 7d. The Great Green Wall of Trees to Halt the Sahara. This project is a prime candidate for support from publicly owned banks. For more detail see pulitzercenter.org/projects/africa-senegal-great-gree n-wall-trees-sahara-desert-sahel

7e. That international efforts be initiated and energetically pursued to address protection of the sea bed, and its possible inclusion as part of the global commons.

Fiscal

8. That creative thinkers investigate alternatives to the current banking system within an ecological economy, that will be fulfilling the traditional roles of banking.

Note 8. This question was raised but not discussed in this text, since it did not appear as a necessary condition for an ecological economy. Nevertheless, the banking system has been very widely criticized, most recently for its contribution to bringing governments, businesses and individuals to the brink of insolvency, and to bankruptcy. It therefore needs to be changed independently of the necessary move toward an ecological economy. Such changes might best have the fully ecological economy as their intention.

8a. That creative thinkers study the choices for coordinating the funding of wealth-creating programs in large single-currency areas.

Note 8a. See Chapter Six

Investment

9. That researchers and lawmakers explore the structures that would effectively prevent publicly owned facilities that are of central importance—such as water purification and distribution facilities—from being sold to private investors for their profit.

Note 9. This recommendation follows from Chapter Five

9a. That researchers and lawmakers investigate public ownership with a view to identifying shareholders in such ownership and upholding meaningful shareholder guarantees.

Note 9a. This recommendation follows from Chapter Five

Businesses

10. For all those who live in a jurisdiction that doesn't have benefit corporations or their equivalent, to lobby for legislation that will open that legal channel.

Note 10. See Chapter Thirteen

10a. Encourage articles in the press about the advantages of benefit corporations.

Government-corporate relations

11. That work begin forthwith on the *Carta Magna*.

Note 11. Chapter Nineteen explains the need for a *Carta Magna*, which arose from gradually increasing corporate dominance through a divide-and-conquer process. This in turn was made possible by nations seeing each other as in competition for scarce benefits. Under the new banner of cooperation, a sustainable civilization and justice for all will more easily be attained.

Appendix 1

The Earth and Its Climate

Climate change is the greatest threat to life in general and the human race in particular and is thus the prime reason for this book, even if the theme is that of ecological economics. So let's look at the Earth's climate, with a quick glance at its history, and try to understand why specific action is urgently needed.

For hundreds of millions of years, Earth has had relatively stable climate in one of two modes: the warm ages, in which there were no ice caps at the poles; and the cool ages, with ice caps. About 252 million years ago, Earth was in a cool age, called the Permian, but a succession of natural causes put a tremendous volume of greenhouse gases into the atmosphere, driving the climate into a warm age, known as the Triassic, without ice caps.

A greenhouse gas (ghg) is one that absorbs infrared radiation emitted from the Earth's surface, thus preventing some of that radiation from reaching outer space. It thus traps heat that, had it escaped, would have kept the average surface temperature roughly constant.

For well over a million years, the Earth has been in a cold age, including numerous ice ages within the overall cool climate. And then, about 200 years ago, humanity started to put large amounts of carbon dioxide into the atmosphere. Initially it came from factories burning coal, and from domestic hearths, trains and steamships but, during the 20th century, it became the oil rush, with oil, natural gas and coal contributing to the total. The primary greenhouse gas is therefore carbon dioxide, CO_2, though other gases are also important, for example methane (when it escapes the Earth's surface unburned) and the oxides of nitrogen, which are formed when carbon fuels are burned in air at high temperatures.

The Earth's reaction to such an atmospheric change is moderately fast on a geological timescale but, when looked at on our human timescale, we can easily fail to grasp delayed effects. So it is easy to say, "Well it isn't really making much difference."

Putting a few thousand megatonnes of CO_2 into the atmosphere has, of itself, a modest enough effect on the balance between energy reaching the Earth's surface and the heat radiated back into space; but the delayed effects can continue for centuries. One delayed effect is the melting of glaciers and ice sheets. These reflect a great deal of the sunlight incident upon them, which is what keeps the Earth cool in an ice age. Once the ice is gone, the sunlight is strongly absorbed by land or water. Other delayed processes include the emission of methane when the Arctic warms. The methane can come from the sea bed or the tundra. Processes of this sort are called feedbacks, since they are not the primary causes of warming, but are triggered at different points during the warming. When a feedback adds to the warming it is termed a positive feedback. When it counters the warming, as is the case when the added CO_2 increases photosynthesis, it is termed negative feedback. Most climate feedbacks are positive. A question then arises: by how much will the feedbacks, given enough time, multiply the warming directly due to the CO_2 emissions?

Until 2013, though climate science had made great progress in identifying and estimating the effects of feedbacks, the total effect of all feedbacks had not been quantified. In 2013, David Wasdell disclosed his finding four points in Earth's history, widely spread in atmospheric CO_2 content, where the global temperatures could be estimated, and where the climate appears to have become stable, which implies that the feedbacks had all produced their full effects [1]. Three of these are plotted in fig. A1.1, the fourth being far off scale to the right of the diagram. Note that the abscissa (the scale of CO_2 concentration) is a semilog plot. Thus, the relationship between heating directly due to the CO_2 (the line of low slope), and the total heating (the steeper line) follow essentially the same relationship. The temperature scale takes its zero from the time of the onset of the industrial revolution, the origin, O, in the diagram. Wasdell has recently pointed out that the point O is not a benchmark for this plot, as are the other points, because it is not a point of equilibrium in the climate [2]. Rather, it falls coincidentally on the line through those other points.

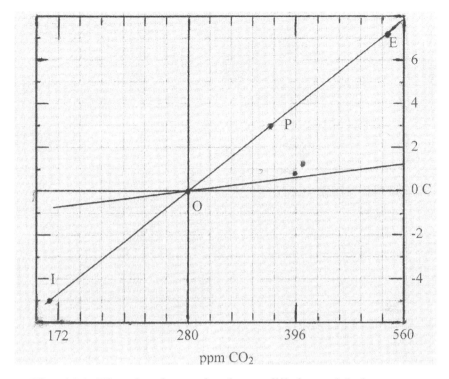

Fig. A1.1. The plot shows the the equilibrium global temperature as a function of carbon dioxide content of the atmosphere. The low-sloping line is what climate models project from added carbon alone, while the steeper line includes the effect of all feedbacks (implicit from the equilibria). Both plots are slightly nonlinear, because the abscissa is a slowly increasing exponential function of the atmospheric carbon content. Each division on the CO_2 scale is seven percent wider than the division to its left. The points on the steeper line are:

I: the lowest ice age point [180, -5.0];

E: the Engelbeen point [534, 7.1]; P: the Pagani point [360, 3.0];

O: a preindustrial reference point [280,0].

The point just above the lower line at the 396 ppm level indicates where the globe was in 2012. The nearby point at 405 ppm concentration indicates where it is today (2017).

The point at 396 ppm of CO_2 in fig. A1.1 lies just above the line of lower slope (no feedbacks) which lies at 0.6 C warming at that concentration. The much steeper line, however, shows a 3.9 C warming at that concentration, suggesting that feedbacks contribute 85 percent to the warming! Because the two lines have constant slopes, the 85 percent would apply at any given CO_2 concentration. Extending our view to the point at 405 ppm (for 2017) it is clear the feedbacks have started to produce their effects, which include further ghg emissions, which in turn increase the atmospheric carbon content and also the expected equilibrium temperature. It is not known how long it would take to reach an equilibrium. Nowadays, it is more usual to talk in terms of climate sensitivity, which means the global temperature rise corresponding to a doubling of the CO_2 content of the atmosphere. Fig. A1.1 would place this just below 8 C, where the steeper line intersects the vertical frameline at 560 ppm.

In the matter of political and social action to address climate change, the climate sensitivity used at international meetings is closer to 3 C, and clearly underestimates the total expected warming, thus maintaining the vain hope of preventing a 2 C rise in global temperature. As of today, fig. A1.1 shows clearly that a 5 C rise will surely be exceeded, unless dramatic and effective measures are taken very soon, a fact that should logically propel the international community to emergency action.

In Wasdell's 2013 talk to the Club of Rome, he presented much of the above, and concluded:

> We have a global emergency on our hands; the emissions from fossil-fuel burning must be reduced to zero by about 2070; and much carbon dioxide already in the atmosphere must be removed from it [1].

A transition

Why is a transition from a generally cool age to a generally warm age, without ice caps, to be avoided? And here we have only one answer: that the transition of 252 million years ago, "The Permian-Triassic," caused the greatest extinction of species in Earth's records. It resembles the transition the human race is now set upon, in that its ghg emissions (which back then came from natural causes) followed the same sort of magnitudes as ours, though more slowly.

A result of greatly increased carbon dioxide in the atmosphere is its diffusion into the ocean, creating carbonic acid. The extinctions must have arisen as follows, that the ocean eventually became acidic to the point it stopped producing oxygen, and this killed off most of marine life. Much plant life, including trees also disappeared during the Permian extinctions, and this was likely due to the emission of hydrogen sulfide from the ocean.

> Life on land depends on a living ocean.

So it is not the warming *per se* that will kill off mammal life and much else, but the near-death of the ocean, which provides most of the oxygen we breathe. And acidification of the ocean is something the climate deniers cannot refute. The ocean has already become significantly less alkaline because of its absorption of CO_2, a process that urgently needs to be halted. And very many ocean species have become extinct since the industrial revolution began, many times the natural rate for such extinctions. It has been announced this year (2017) that Australia's great Barrier Reef is dying, an appalling tragedy in the making. Meanwhile the acidification is accelerating, while the ghg emissions globally are still on the increase.

Eliminating emissions is a matter of survival, not economic convenience!

A point of no return?

Wasdell has also devised a method of telling whether we have reached a point of no return in the transition to a generally warm climate without ice caps [1]. Passing the point of no return would mean that climate warming would continue regardless of burning of fossil fuels in the human economy. Nevertheless, he said, we still have time, a real reason for optimism; but we have no reason for complacency or delay. We are most uncomfortably close to that point of no return.

Notes

1. Adapted from Wasdell 2013 webcast from the Club of Rome: <onsync.digitalsamba.com/play/wasdell/14146-cor-dw-keynote>.

2. David Wasdell private communication 2017

Appendix 2

Important projections

Chapter One and Appendix 1 have, it is to be hoped, convinced some readers that we really don't have much time to put things right in the domain of climate change. And the task is huge. Therefore, anything that diverts or delays human attention from this task could be fatal in the long term. The collapse of civilization is an immediate global example, since the institutions and governance of civilization will be needed for the huge collective effort of humans to remove the climate threat.

In *The Collapse of Complex Societies* (1988), Joseph Tainter tells us not only about the reasons for collapse of past civilizations, but of identifiable stages in the process. In Jared Diamond's work, *Collapse* (2005), he examines the process in various states and empires, and includes examples of a few island societies that managed to avoid collapse. Ronald Wright, in *A Brief History of Progress* (2004) pegs his accounts of collapse on three phrases borrowed from Tainter, which describe two conditions leading to collapse and finally the collapse itself. These are the runaway train, the dinosaur factor; and the house of cards. Wright sees the runaway train of our own civilization as being due to population increase, the acceleration of technology, the concentration of wealth and power, and the hemorrhage of waste. Somehow the depleting capital resources got left out, but they are implicit, and he is really stating that, with ruling power concentrated in too few hands, you can't enact a new system that would protect capital resources.

The dinosaur factor today is obvious: crucially important national leaders not recognizing that we are following typical behavior of past failed civilizations.

The house of cards, the collapse itself cannot be predicted, but one of the useful indicators is likely to be the state of the world's forests, since our woods are the keepers of water, and past civilizations that failed to preserve their forests collapsed, so we shall look briefly at the prospects for forest, globally.

To provide a timescale for the kind of urgency we face, three projections are presented here, all relevant to this century and the period within which we must regulate our behavior vis-à-vis the ghg emissions and climate change in general. The first two resulted from a computer program called Global Systems Simulator (GSS). The program is a modeling tool that integrates economic stocks and throughput globally. It was developed by Robert Hoffman, a professional economist and modeler running a modeling business in Ottawa; he is also a member of the Club of Rome. The GSS is used to show limits and trends, without breakdown into the economics of regions or individual countries. It uses only physical units for assessing resources, not money. At two of the international roundtables of the Global Issues Project [1], Robert Hoffman made the GSS available to demonstrate projecting scarcities, with the following results:

1) Forests. Under assumptions of *laissez-faire*, which means economics and attitudes as at the time of these studies (2005-2009), a severe *tension* will arise in the world's forest sector by the year 2038. The word *tension* here means that supply will fall short of demand. There'll be a marked shortage of lumber. Only immature, small-diameter trees will be available worldwide. Such a situation will have arisen because of overcutting, illegal cutting and deliberate burning of forest over many decades, all of which are continuing as I write (2017). The plundering of tropical rainforests in some countries has been known for many years, notwithstanding persistent international efforts at conservation of these vital resources. The effects of excessive harvesting can be seen in many other places – for example, in New Brunswick and Nova Scotia, Canada, where the age distribution of trees is very heavily slanted toward young trees, and mature trees amount to a very tiny fraction of the total. We used Hoffman's GSS twice to look at the forest sector, several years apart, obtaining the date 2038 for the tension onset both times. On the second occasion, the input data were much more recent than the first, so that the two results thus corresponded to a span of more than three years. The results suggest that the world (including those who cut lumber

illegally) has not recognized the danger of loss of forest. Cutting worldwide, legal plus illegal, follows demand and far exceeds what is sustainable. Overcutting is thus widespread, though some jurisdictions manage to limit cutting to sustainable levels within their boundaries.

2) We also used the GSS in 2009 to assess world population, for which the model requires current population figures, average birth rates, death rates, information on agriculture (available land for agriculture and its fertility), and so on. The model then projects the future food output and global population, not excluding the possibility of famine. Given a complete set of inputs, and again assuming economic *laissez-faire*, we arrived at an age of global food tension by the year 2040, resulting in a peaking of population between 2040 and 2050, the onset of the decline being presumed to arise from famine. Since there are already several areas of the world that experience severe (life-threatening) food shortage, and the world's agricultural land area is decreasing annually, while global population continues to increase, it appeared clear to us that a critical *global* food shortage must soon occur, unless new developments in food production or changes in population growth take place soon enough. The GSS enabled us to determine that with present trends and knowledge, the global food tension would occur in that decade, under *laissez-faire*. An early cessation of population growth, which is surely possible, would markedly change our projected data, as might breakthroughs in food production.

Lastly there's the work of twelve oceanographers [2], who estimate the end of commercial fishing of wild ocean fish at 2048, by which time they projected there will be too few fish of any size suitable for commerce to make it worthwhile for any fishing boat to set out to sea. In the meantime, there will be an increase in fish farming, but we have no way of attempting to predict its output.

Joel Bourne Jr, however, has published an important and thorough study of food production and its likely future trends, *The End of Plenty*

(2015). This work faces up to the probable nine billion people to be fed in the 2040s. Though Bourne admits some pessimism, he sees a few possibilities for increase in food production. Fish farming, especially, may be entering a new age for production without ocean pollution.

To conclude these dreary projections, the human race can only expect horrendous shortages and their social consequences under *laissez-faire*, and the projected dates for these immense *tensions*, when last examined, lay between 2038 and 2048.

Evidently, *laissez-faire* isn't good enough.

Notes

1. The Global Issues Project is a group founded by three scholars, which grew to eleven members during the years 2005-12, and sponsored seven international roundtables on crucial issues, each time with well-known cosponsoring partners. The material in this appendix contains some output from these roundtables.

2. B Worm et al. "Impacts of biodiversity loss on ecosystem services" *Science* **314** (2006) pp. 9884-9888.

Appendix 3

Ecological Footprint

This appendix presents the basis of assessment of the impact of societies (nations) upon their territories, from the standpoint of sustainability. Is the nature of a nation's territory and waters such that these can sustain the population and absorb the pollution produced by human activities as they are? A valuable source of information on how the world is doing in such respects is provided by "Footprint News":

(www.footprintnetwork.org/resources) online, based on the concept of ecological footprint.

The concept of footprint is so important that readers unfamiliar with it will need to understand it. It was introduced in 1992 by Bill Rees, a professor now retired from the University of British Columbia [1]. He was joined by a graduate student, Mathis Wackernagel, and together they explored the concept and refined it [2]. Today, Wackernagel is President of the Global Footprint Network with offices in Oakland, Brussels and Geneva, and a staff of nineteen including himself. The results of their findings are published through the internet, in their "Footprint News" [3], and their website.

During the past 25 years, the evaluation of footprint has become increasingly sophisticated and accurate. Along with the study of footprint (the impact humanity has on its territory and waters) they evaluate *biocapacity*—the ability of their land and waters to supply human needs and absorb human pollution. Both the footprint and the biocapacity of a nation can be expressed as areas, the biocapacity being what one has to sustain life, while the footprint is what one would need to have to live sustainably. If the footprint exceeds the biocapacity, that society is living beyond its ecological means, either by extravagance or through its too large population. If the footprint is smaller than the biocapacity, all is well, at least for now.

There can be slight confusion here as footprint is often referred to as the ratio of two areas, while immediately above it is defined as an area.

Perhaps the ratio should be called specific footprint, or sustainability indicator, without dimensions (a bit like relative humidity), but its not difficult to bear with the ambiguity.

During the development of footprint studies, results have been criticized on various grounds at various times [4]. New evaluations and definitions of footprint have also been created by numerous researchers, so that the literature is full of rich findings [4]. But, for our purposes, Wackernagel's "Footprint News" will serve us very well because it provides the following vital information. First, it tells us how the world is doing ecologically, as a whole and also nation by nation. Second, it tells us what kinds of activities are contributing to the footprint sector by economic sector, so that ministries, municipalities, other authorities, corporations, businesses, institutions and individuals can take appropriate action. Third, it tells us the aggregate global footprint, which for almost five decades has been in the overshoot mode, meaning that we are using resources future generations will need, or that we are polluting more than the Earth system can tolerate.

Footprint layer-cake diagram

The layer-cake diagram shows how the footprint derives from various sectors of the economy. It can be viewed in color at

www.footprintnetwork.org/resources

by scrolling to Data and Insights and clicking on DIVE INTO DATA, which displays a full-color diagram titled, "World ecological Footprint by Component." This is the "layer-cake" diagram. The fattest component is colored in blue and represents carbon put into the atmosphere. The horizontal axis is the year. For 2012, the blue band contributes 58 percent of the total footprint. If those carbon emissions were zero, all of them, not just those from fossil-fuel burning, the global footprint for 2012 would have been down to 0.68, well within the sustainable level of 1.0. Here I am using the ratio of footprint to biocapacity.

Footprint nation by nation

On the same site, one may scroll down to Country Trends, where there is a colored global map showing the footprints nation by nation, the deepest red indicating those nations with the highest ecological footprint relative to biocapacity

As stated above, greenhouse gas emissions make an enormous contribution to the global footprint. If only the emissions from fossil-fuel burning were reduced to zero, the global footprint would stand close to 1.0, on the threshold of sustainability. However, there are a few countries where the population has reached such a high level that even the elimination of ghg emissions would not bring their national footprint down to 1.0.

A global footprint of 1.0 would imply some countries are above that important threshold, and others below it.

Notes

1. Rees, William E (October 1992) "Ecological footprints and appropriated carrying capacity: what urban economics leaves out" *Environment and Urbanization 4 (2): 121–130.*doi:10.1177/095624789200400212

2. Wackernagel, Mathis and William Rees *Our Ecological Footprint* New Society Press 1996.

3. Global Footprint Network · 312 Clay Street, Suite 300 · Oakland, CA 94607-3510 · USA

4. Wikipedia "Ecological Footprint"

Appendix 4

Biochar and Climate Change

Tom Miles writes [1] "I would characterize biochar in North America as having a small but growing industrial and commercial presence and a very active academic community. About 140 companies in North America are producing and marketing biochar, primarily for higher value retail garden, horticultural, and environmental (storm water, remediation) applications. The delivered cost of biochar is generally high for broad agriculture although growers are finding ways to use small amounts of char effectively. Large quantities of biochar are produced as co-products at wood and bioenergy plants. We are seeing small plants that are primarily producing biochar.

"Internationally, biochar is finding use in restoring degraded land and improving smallholder agriculture in developing countries, especially in China, Korea, Japan and SE Asia. China and now the Philippines have large government sponsored programs to use biochar to remediate degraded agricultural and mine land. IBI opened IBI-Asia at the Nanjing Agricultural University in October 2016 where they have an active biochar research and field station." [2]

Biochar enthusiasts have long maintained that biochar will greatly assist in addressing climate change through increased sequestration of carbon dioxide from the air by plants grown in the more fertile soil that has been treated with biochar [3]. This is very likely true, and the potential for additional sequestration is considerable, though the benefit is achieved at a price, namely, that carbon dioxide is emitted when the biochar is produced. Biochar is made by heating organic matter in a closed oven into which no air is fed, but there's enough oxygen within the organic matter to produce about as many CO_2 molecules as there are carbon atoms left in the biochar. The question then is, which wins in the long term? The answer is sequestration, but there's an interval of years before the quantity of CO_2 emitted is recovered, and the time taken goes inversely as the difference in fertility gain by putting biochar into the soil. Thus, biochar as a means of sequestration works best if very infertile land is made fertile [4].

Notes

1. Tom Miles private communication 2 April 2017
2. International Biochar Initiative (IBI) www.biochar-international.org
3. Dominic Woolf, James Amonette, Alayne Street-Perrot, Joseph Lehmann and Stephen Joseph "Sustainable Biochar to Mitigate Global Climate Change" *Nature Communications* **1** article 56 2010.
4. Derek Paul "Biochar-enhanced Sequestration of Atmospheric Carbon Dioxide" presented at the September 2010 Roundtable on Biochar in Toronto and published in the *SfP Bulletin* October 2010. www.scienceforpeace.ca

Appendix 5

Threats of Extinction of Wild Life

The story of the extinctions of wild life resulting from human folly or negligence is long, sad and already old. Today the story continues, but much more starkly now through the shrinking of habitat, due to developments arising from the huge numbers of people in almost all habitable areas of the planet. Human expansion began long ago, but on a small enough scale that it was easy to ignore until recently.

Extinctions caused by the human race are pertinent to the discussion of population, partly because they reveal the difficulty of retaining biodiversity in a world overcrowded with people, but also because some such stories continue to reveal human thoughtlessness and worse, deliberate slaughter through lack of understanding of our proper relationship with the biosphere. The aboriginal people of North America never killed animals unnecessarily. They had learned through the experience of thousands of years that all were interdependent.

The 19th century exterminations are legion. They include the great awk, which was willfully exterminated by sailors for no reason other than their perverse pleasure. In 1800 the passenger pigeon throve in millions, but they were found to be good to eat, and their numbers declined, especially rapidly between 1870 and 1890, until the species was clearly threatened. The slaughter nevertheless continued until the last individual died in a zoo in 1914. Mammals are prominent in the long list of exterminations. Somehow, a few plains bison got preserved following willful destruction of millions of them in the 19th century. Of the bison family in North America today, only the wood bison have their own, protected territory and can live in the wild. The determination to kill for sport continues, with immense pressure on governments to allow killing of wolves where they exist in the wild. An approximation to the truth for surviving species in 2017 is that all wild mammals are threatened with extinction, for environmental reasons including loss of habitat, or because they are hunted for trophies, as is the case for tigers, elephants and rhinoceros, or for fun, or a combination of the foregoing.

Birds especially have declined tremendously in numbers this last half century, from loss of habitat and several other human-related causes. These latter include chemical pollution and deaths from cutting of forest during the nesting season. Smaller birds suffer tremendous losses from domestic cats, and significant losses in collisions with tall buildings and modern windmills, all of which are, in principle, preventable. The enormous annual loss of birds due to domestic cats is related to the human population, and is thus some kind of measure of human overpopulation.

Species in the ocean are no less under threat. First it was whales, then cod, now sharks and all other species, especially if edible. Trawling in the ocean increases the efficiency of the catch and proportionally the rate of loss of numbers remaining in the ocean, which can lead to extinction. There are UN mechanisms to help stop the decline, but these do not yet seem to be sufficiently effective.

In the ocean also, huge numbers of species become extinct when a coral reef dies. Such reefs die from pollution, accelerated by ocean warming and decreasing alkalinity of the water. Loss of alkalinity of the ocean is important more generally, and is a prime reason that fossil fuels should no longer be burned. The state of the world's remaining coral is a sensitive measure of human destruction of the ecosphere, and it is now known (2017) that the famous and wonderful Australian Great Barrier Reef is dying.

The Living Planet Index established that, on average, species declined in their numbers by 25 percent from 1970 to 2000 [1]. Assuming an exponential decay, this represents almost 1.2 percent decline per year.

Note

1. Jonathan Loh et al. 2005 DOI:10.1098/rsto.2004.1584

About the author

Derek Paul is a retired physicist who has also published in several other fields. He obtained his Bachelor's degree from Cambridge University and then worked for three years in industry. In 1953 he took up residence in Kingston, Ontario teaching and doing research in atomic physics for a decade at the Royal Military College of Canada. He obtained a doctorate from Queens University in 1958. From 1964-95 he was a professor at the University of Toronto. In 1976 he became a participant in the Pugwash Conferences on Science and World Affairs, with their focus on peace issues. The Soviet invasion of Afghanistan in December 1979 and the maximum tension in the Cold War greatly changed his off-duty activities, which came to include co-founding Science for Peace (1981), and several visits to the Soviet Union and one to East Germany, all on peace matters. In 2005, he cofounded the Global Issues Project which grew to a committee of eleven and organized international roundtables over seven years on crucial issues spanning forests, climate change, fresh water, food, population, a no-growth economy, biochar, and peace in outer space. He wrote this book because of the urgent need for a new economic system that would enable the world to address the huge threat of climate change. He is a member of two physical societies and of the International Society for Ecological Economics.

Index

Printed in Great Britain
by Amazon